CJTF—A Lifeline for a European Defence Policy?

Edited by
Edward Foster and Gordon Wilson

Royal United Services Institute for Defence Studies

First Published 1997

© Royal United Services Institute for Defence Studies

ISBN 0-85516-165-5
ISSN 0268-1307

The Royal United Services Institute for Defence Studies (RUSI) is a professional body based in London dedicated to the study, analysis and debate of issues affecting defence and international security.

Founded in 1831 by the Duke of Wellington, the RUSI is one of the most senior institutes of its kind in the world which, throughout its history, has been at the forefront of contemporary political-military thinking through debates, public and private seminars, conferences, lectures and a wide range of publications. The independence of the Institute is guaranteed by a large, worldwide membership of those people and organisations who have a serious and professional interest in the thorough and objective analysis of defence and international security.

Critical and acclaimed analysis of issues of the moment has underwritten the RUSI's Whitehall Papers for many years. The new series will, in its revised A5 monograph format, continue to provide expertise in the field. The series, which will comprise six publications a year, will address the major areas of current interest.

Whitehall Papers are available as part of a membership package, or singly at £6.50 plus p & p (£1.00 in the UK/£2.00 overseas). Orders should be sent to the Publications Department, RUSI, Whitehall, London SW1A 2ET and cheques and postal orders made payable to the RUSI.

Printed in Great Britain by Sherrens Printers, Units 1 & 2, South Park, Granby Industrial Estate, Weymouth, Dorset.
The Royal United Services Institute for Defence Studies, Whitehall, London SW1A 2ET.
Registered Charity No. 210639

CONTENTS

NOTE ON THE TEXT

This Whitehall Paper brings together papers given at a conference jointly organised by RUSI and the WEU Institute for Security Studies and held at the WEU Institute in Paris in April 1997.

Edward Foster is Head of RUSI's European Programme. Captain Gordon Wilson RN is a Researcher at the WEU Institute for Security Studies.

INTRODUCTION:
CJTF—A LIFELINE FOR A EUROPEAN DEFENCE POLICY?

The title chosen for the seminar, which the WEU Institute for Strategic Studies jointly organised with RUSI, appropriately conveys, with just a slightly theatrical touch, the gist of what has become the most topical issue in European security politics. Devised after the end of the Cold War, the Combined Joint Task Force (CJTF) concept is not only about the mechanics of NATO's operational reform. It is also, fundamentally, about maintaining the meaning of the transatlantic link in the new international circumstances. Increasing NATO's effectiveness implies improving its flexibility; this, in turn, requires more committed and diversified European contributions.

Operational capability cannot be dissociated from political credibility: they must remain a function of each other, as the European security system evolves and adapts to events whose nature and configuration defy the capability of institutions to rationalise and control them. As transition affects every country, big or small, the prevention of causes, rather than containment of consequences, is a widespread concern. Crisis management must be tailored to individual situations as they manifest themselves. No alliance or other international agreement can provide ready-made commitments to cope with the multifaceted and ambiguous contingencies that lie ahead, in non-Article Five situations (setting aside therefore collective territorial defence). Security, whether domestic or international, is more than ever a question of predictability, transparency, accountability and democratic involvement. It is managers rather than architects that are needed, as existing European security institutions must be disentangled. In the words of NATO Secretary-General Javier Solana, 'it is a matter of synergies, not hierarchies'.

A re-empowering of Europe with new responsibilities and capabilities is thus on the international agenda, not only because history is knocking again at Europe's door, but also because it is in the best interest of the

1

United States. The US has inextricably become a European power. It is the common denominator of every European national foreign policy; it will continue to be the essential coalition-builder (the stuff of which leadership is made nowadays). But the US cannot substitute for the pluralistic, converging effort that complex contingencies require. Washington's approach will remain for the foreseeable future the indispensable catalyst in Europe's transition, but its stabilising role cannot succeed single-handedly. Conceivably, the most coherent outcome should consist of the combination of a more adjustable operational NATO structure, through the CJTF mechanism, with greater solidarity in European foreign policy achieved through the gradual enactment of the Maastricht vision. The Amsterdam and Madrid summits of the EU and NATO will provide the parameters for this. The Western European Union (WEU) will naturally find itself at the intersection of the two reform processes, as the instrument of either a downsized NATO mission or an enhanced EU task. Consequently, whatever the final institutional outcome of their separate introspective processes, NATO, EU and WEU must improve their respective interrelationships for the purposes of improving their political credibility and accountability, in the context of Europe's policy of integration.

In November and December 1991, with the adoption of NATO's New Strategic Concept and the EU's Maastricht Treaty, the two organisations simultaneously reinforced the political dimension to their integrated structures, most conspicuously military and economic. Their generous competition in projecting stability to Central and Eastern Europe must not inadvertently produce conflicting strategies between NATO and the EU. Recent events have shown that the US and Europe adopt a different approach to crisis management. Washington needs to be militarily decisive, with clear-cut engagement and exit strategies, but Congress balks at putting the lives of American GIs at stake on the ground. On the other hand, the Europeans take a humanitarian perspective and prefer to engage in civilian involvement in the field. The two attitudes are by no means alternative or contradictory; in future, they will need to become more complementary.

Clearly, on the whole Europe must establish itself as a more coherent actor and increasingly take upon itself a variety of roles. Burden-sharing must include responsibility- and task-sharing. The US needs to co-opt and involve, not substitute, lest it discourage the still hesitant reappropriation of responsibilities by the Europeans. In 1994 NATO formally acknowledged the existence of a European Security and Defence Identity (ESDI) in its midst, and, at its Berlin ministerial, approved the Combined Joint Task Force concept, designating the WEU as the body responsible for the political control and strategic direction of ('separable but not separate') European missions. The EU Intergovernmental Conference, in the meantime, prepared for the inclusion of the so-called Petersberg tasks into the revised EU Treaty. The WEU need not choose between these two suitors. In practice, it will have to take political sustenance from the EU and operational support from NATO, whenever the latter does not take matters upon itself.

In order to deal with the varied and ambiguous challenges of today, no single approach will suffice. In many instances, coalitions of the willing will prove more effective than any institutional posturing. A bottom-up pragmatic approach will have to emerge and be allowed to develop, reaching upwards for the indispensable top-down institutional legitimation. It is this combination that will produce the necessary linkage between political credibility and operational effectiveness. Some disentangling of existing institutions may therefore prove helpful: in non-Article Five contingencies, should NATO and the WEU be linked like Siamese twins or could their European memberships continue to differ? For the same purpose, should applicants for EU membership be made to wait until they meet the economic convergence criteria of the EU's first Pillar, before they are allowed to partake in the political consultation and planning of Pillars II and III? Could not the Council of Europe and the OSCE be provided with more incisive tasks in producing solidarity and compatibility?

In the changing European security environment, and in order to encourage broader European involvement on a continental scale, the implications of CJTF transcend their operational significance: they have become a political tool, at the very core of transatlantic relations. The consultative process established by Article Four of the Washington Treaty must be brought to the fore, alongside the collective defence of Article Five, with a reapportioning of responsibilities, both political and military, and improved coordination. With or without CJTF, North Americans and Europeans must motivate each other to undertake different but compatible responsibilities, in response to the aspirations of the new European democracies and the world at large. In any case, the fledgling Common Foreign and Security Policy (CFSP) of the EU should soon define its profile (including the ESDI that NATO has accepted) instead of waiting for NATO to concede it. The Transatlantic Alliance would be reinforced, not weakened, by it.

Ambassador Guido Lenzi
Director, WEU Institute for Strategic Studies

******

Combined Joint Task Forces themselves are nothing new; even the name is not quite new. The various armed forces of different nations have long joined together in common cause, most notably perhaps in the Second World War, and the D-Day landings are a supreme example. But using that sort of combination was how many of the unfought campaigns of the Cold War were planned and exercised, so NATO has also long embraced the idea in its broadest form. What is new is the particular arrangement postulated at NATO's Brussels summit in 1994, whereby the European allies could act militarily under European command and draw upon certain assets and capabilities owned by other non-European nations of the Alliance (in practice the United States).

The reason why this comparatively straightforward military arrangement is linked to the idea of a life-line for a European Defence Policy is rooted in the resurgence of the WEU in the last years of the Cold War and in the characteristics of the disordered multi-polar world in which we all found ourselves after the collapse of the Soviet Union. NATO had to evolve and it was plainly in the interest of both Europe and the United States for the European pillar of the Alliance to be more autonomous, more effective and preferably stronger. The CFSP, created but not given substance under the Maastricht Treaty, is supposed to lead in due course to a common defence policy and then to a common defence. But the road from one to the other is long and bumpy, and there have to be some sustainable and useful stations along the way. Furthermore, the collapse of the threat from the Soviet Union has understandably, but in some disregard of the instability all around, led to an unwillingness by the Europeans to maintain defence spending at the level of the latter Cold War years, still less to increase it. At the same time, the nature of warfare has been evolving in concert with the strategic environment, and this has added emphasis to the value of certain capabilities, systems and platforms. Consequently, there is no sensible prospect of the European Alliance nations, either singly or together, reproducing the capabilities gained from use of collective Alliance or United States systems.

Even given full coordination of political and military will amongst participating European nations, perhaps acting on behalf of the WEU, certain gaps in military capabilities and assets will be evident for all but the lowest level military tasks. It is true that the Petersberg tasks which the Europeans plan to undertake alone are essentially at a low level and can be grouped loosely under the heading of humanitarian and peace-keeping operations. If all goes according to plan, the capabilities, assets and numbers of the European armed forces, acting in concert, should be adequate. But there are complications.

Low-level conflicts often do not follow the expected dynamics of current politico-military planning, and whether this is because our understanding of low level conflict is imperfect, or whether we have to accept that these conflicts respond to chaotic and unpredictable influences, the likelihood remains that what starts off as an apparently small and manageable problem may well escalate in intensity, scope and geographic coverage, and extend in time. Thus, before becoming committed to one of the low-level tasks, the Europeans need to have contingency plans on how to cope with this escalation and expansion in such a way that the conduct of the operation does not suffer a hiatus whilst new arrangements are put together. The phrase 'escalation dominance' is used to describe this process which needs to link seamlessly, and under control, the conduct of a small localised operation towards the engagement of the full panoply of NATO's military might. If this can be seen to be achievable, both politically and militarily, then this may have a dampening or deterrent effect on the original antagonists. If it cannot, then the temptation to escalate a conflict beyond the capability of the Europeans and into an area where there is, with whatever logic, a prospect of a better outcome, may prove irresistible.

But 'escalation dominance' is not the only reason for the Europeans to want access to Alliance or US assets. Some of the systems involved, for surveillance or command and control, are force-multipliers: they enable troops, ships and aircraft to undertake their missions much more effectively and more cost-effectively. In other words, they enable the Europeans to undertake their tasks better, even before any escalation occurs. Much the same can be said of capabilities such as strategic transport, which may extend the reach and endurance of the core European capabilities. These same Alliance capabilities have a further advantage in that they will tend to reduce European casualties, thus increasing the resilience of the political cohesion in and between participating states. They may also reduce collateral casualties, which, apart from the direct humanitarian benefit, will reduce the opportunities for escalation, duplicity and antagonism towards would-be peacekeepers.

Thus the CJTF concept should, when implemented, enable the Europeans to undertake the range of lower level military tasks they deem appropriate effectively, securely, and affordably. It will give military muscle to emerging European Defence Policies that will allow European states to aspire to a military capability proportionate to their aggregated size and economic strength. If it is judged that Europe, without CJTFs, would flounder amid hand-wringing platitudes and economic sanctions, then CJTFs are truly a life-line for a European Defence Policy. Being one lifeline does not deny the possibility of there being others. It is simply that other convincing examples do not seem to have been found yet.

The concept is not, however, without its drawbacks. Let us, for a moment, consider just the United States-owned assets. However well-intentioned and generous the Americans may be at the beginning of a task, however much they may hand over the levers of command at the operational and tactical levels of command, they will still retain 'full command' of their forces assigned to European missions. This means they can still pull the plug on any operation, on any pretext which is convincing to them and at any time. This would have a most unwelcome and disruptive effect on the conduct of the mission, both militarily and politically. Moreover, just as there should be 'no taxation without representation', there must be at least a grumbling undercover feeling in Washington that there should be no military participation without a voice in the policies of implementation. Such a voice could be audible beneath the parapet of public awareness through diplomatic channels, but it would have force nonetheless. The fear in Europe might be that, whatever assurances are given, the European military autonomy will, in the last resort, have the Damoclean sword of an American political veto hanging over it. This in turn could give rise to perceptions among other parties that an appeal to the Americans over the heads of the Europeans would always be possible, and that given enough hubbub, the Europeans might not have the stomach to see the mission through to a conclusion. On the other hand, one might suggest that this just institutionalises the present economic, political and strategic realities.

There is a sub-set of the arguments that is worth noting. American politicians, public and military will be asked to accept that command of American forces in conflict is given up to officers of other nations. This is a significant departure. Whilst most Americans thus engaged will not be exposed to any fighting, there is a risk that, say, the pilot of a strategic lift aircraft might be killed. However insignificant that event might be in the context of a domestic traffic accident and urban violence statistics, it will have a major effect on United States public opinion: witness the roar of patriotic fervour that erupted when a US Air Force pilot was shot down over Banja Luka in June 1995. This may be a strength or a weakness in the American psyche, but it has to be taken into account.

The CJTF concept is being pulled two ways: by a need to preserve and purify the Europeaness of the arrangements and by the requirement to safeguard American interests without direct control. There is a danger in all this that a negotiated compromise may be too convoluted, too strait-jacketed, to work effectively and flexibly. Yet CJTFs must do both: effectively, because otherwise CJTFs will be like a flooded ship in a state of loll; flexibly, because that is clearly what the strategic environment demands. The progress of the arrangements through the NATO decision-making machinery continues at a pace of which Nanny would have approved—'Chew forty times before swallowing'—but there is an archaic ring to it all, reminiscent of over-elaborated soft-ware requirements which are articulated so finely that the system will be out of date before it is in service. CJTF has been a long time in gestation, with some way to go. There would be merit, perhaps, in not worrying too much about the completeness of the arrangements down to the last scintilla of sensitivity and in allowing some admittedly imperfect 'rapid prototyping' to go ahead. There is an added layer of caution that those who take real decisions on behalf of the Alliance must observe, but the arrangements for CJTFs are not like decisions that might have broken the mould of the Cold War. The penalties for delay are as daunting as the dangers of haste: the security environment will continue to evolve and anarchic, nihilistic, trans-nationalistic, nationalistic, sub-nationalistic and ethnic forces are moving and interacting; the Alliance itself is evolving and enlarging; and new systems and capabilities are opening up new opportunities. It would be a shame if CJTF were to finish with the ironic epitaph: '*C'est magnifique, mais ce n'est pas la guerre*'.

Some Europeans (and I naturally include the British within this group) use the abbreviations CJTF and ESDI almost interchangeably. But it seems to me to be wrong-headed to try to fit them both, superimposed, into the same template. I prefer to think of them as two-dimensional ellipses moving in a constrained three dimensional space, frequently meeting but rarely coinciding. CJTFs may indeed be a life-line for a European Defence Policy and may be a manifestation of ESDI, but the structural cart must not be put before the policy and conceptual horse. I hope that it can be accepted that the ESDI must be articulated in part through a European Defence Policy and the latter can be given substance through CJTFs. If CJTFs can be a life-line, they will not necessarily be a permanent one, and the European Defence Policy must look additionally to other means of support. Perhaps CJTFs may provide essential fertiliser to a sickly seedling, but cannot alone guarantee a healthy harvest.

The Royal United Services Institute has greatly valued the opportunity to cooperate with the WEU Institute for Strategic Studies not only in planning and implementing our Conference in Paris, but also in producing this Whitehall Paper that gives both an account of the Conference and an independent commentary on a stimulating and important subject. Our speakers and respondents spoke on the record, but there were other useful interventions, from the conference floor or even over a late-night beer, which were unattributable. I hope that this volume provides a fair record of the whole proceedings, and at the same time gives some idea of the light and shade of the two days. I suspect that the circumstances are sufficiently dynamic that this will in retrospect be seen to be a snap-shot of how the inter-relationship of CJTFs and the European Defence Policy looked in the Spring of 1997.

Rear Admiral Richard Cobbold
Director, Royal United Services Institute for Defence Studies

PART I: EUROPEAN STRUCTURES & SECURITY ISSUES

SECURITY STRUCTURES IN TRANSFORMATION: A GLOBAL OVERVIEW
ADAM DANIEL ROTFELD

> *'[Sovereignty] is possible only within the framework of multinational communities, of common institutions designed to provide common responses to common challenges. Security is no longer attainable in the traditional way. Neither the walled city nor the nation-state can provide protection against attack or threats of physical destruction ... Increasingly the politics of nations revolve around the careful management of interdependence.'*[1]

The subject of this paper is the roles played by multilateral security structures in Europe today. I shall not dwell on the mandates and roles of these organisations in the past. Instead I would like to touch upon several issues concerning the evolution of these multilateral structures in the context of changes that are taking place in Europe after the end of the Cold War, and in particular those issues that critically affect the shaping of a new security system in Europe. The reflections of Johan Jørgen Holst, cited above, before his untimely death, are a reminder that, in search of a new security system, states will increasingly be involved in processes of integration and seek to take advantage of multilateral institutions to manage international interdependence. Thus the first item of a future security agenda, as Brian Urquart has observed, must be 'to preserve, rationalise and strengthen the international and multilateral framework that has been built up over the last fifty years'.[2]

Dr Adam Daniel Rotfeld is Director of the Stockholm International Peace Research Institute (SIPRI). This paper is adapted from his contribution to the 1997 SIPRI Yearbook.

The point is that institutions, by their very nature, are static, while security processes are dynamic, particularly in the course of a fundamental restructuring of the entire international system. The conclusion to draw from this is as follows: that the structures which were called into being after the Second World War (such as the United Nations) or during the Cold War (such as NATO and the Western European Union) call for reforms that are adequate to the scale of the radical changes that have altered the security environment. Thus transformed and adapted, these multilateral institutions must respond to new requirements, new policy areas, new competences, and new instruments and decision-making procedures 'for a functional and politically adequate and effective handling of the institutions' list of tasks.'[3]

Regionalism versus globalism

The evolution of a security system is not linear. Since the threats which the security system was to meet in the past have changed fundamentally, its driving forces, dimensions, forms, procedures and mechanisms of operation must consequently also adapt. In the past, the great powers claimed to be 'international security wardens'. Under the bipolar system, the options were limited and non-great powers were obliged to reconcile themselves to the existing state of affairs. In the multi-polar world, small and medium-size states are gaining in significance. In the European context, this finds expression in efforts to strengthen the European pillar of the Euro-Atlantic partnership; notably the EU's Common Foreign and Security Policy (CFSP), the European Security and Defence Identity (ESDI), the Combined Joint Task Forces (CJTF) concept, and other subregional arrangements.

Similarly, domestic factors play an increasing role in shaping international security. This has led Samuel Huntington to a concept of neo-isolationism, expounded in his thesis on a remade world order based on civilisational *realpolitik*: 'In a multipolar, multi-civilisational world, the West's responsibility is to secure its own interests, not to promote those of other peoples when those conflicts are of little or no consequence to the West.'[4] In this form, a concept has been created of immunising the wealthy world—the United States and the West—against the problems that beset the poor countries of Africa, Asia and Latin America. The practical effects of such a construct, were they treated as a point of reference for political action, would lead in the long run to catastrophe, irrespective of whether it occurred as a 'clash of civilisations' (as propounded by Huntington) or confrontation between the rich North and the poor South, as others warn. Security must be based both on common values—the product of history, culture, civilisation, religion or common institutions—and on a community of vital interests—political, economic, military and others. It is these vital interests that largely determine the rules of conduct of states.

NATO and the WEU

The unambiguous identification of potential threats is essential to the effective operation of a military alliance and the proper definition of its mandate. In today's post-Cold War era these threats are unpredictable. The ongoing debate and the decisions made in 1996 reflect an attempt to accommodate NATO and other structures to the new security environment, one which presents no definite enemy or clear-cut threat. In this absence, vaguely-defined terms such as 'uncertainty', 'instability', 'risks' and 'challenges' have characterised the debate. The paradox of the post-Cold War situation is that the old ('bad') military instruments have been transformed with relative ease into new ('good') confidence- and security-building tools. This is easily explained by the fact that military instruments are, on the one hand, available, organised and deployable, while on the other hand, they have lost their excessive political significance.

A key question for the future of the Alliance is that of relations between the United States and its European allies. These are based on the premises that, on the one hand, NATO remains of prime importance to the United States as the foundation of its security engagement in Europe; while, on the other hand, the end of the hegemonic threat to Europe means that the US role will become 'more uncertain and less central'.[5] Although far from isolationist, the United States is becoming increasingly preoccupied with its own domestic priorities and with geostrategic and economic interests in Asia. Since the primary mission of NATO (that is, collective defence under Article Five of the North Atlantic Treaty) has declined in importance and the Alliance has in turn evolved 'into a motor of European security cooperation and a catalyst for political change',[6] the European members of the Alliance have been pursuing the search for a more cohesive and independent European defence pillar, albeit one which does not undermine the US commitment.

In this respect, the decisions taken in the North Atlantic Council (NAC) in Berlin in June 1996 offered to give practical meaning to the WEU Petersberg missions defined in 1992. Concerning the concept of Combined Joint Task Forces (CJTFs), the Berlin decisions were highly symbolic:

> 'By permitting a more flexible and mobile deployment of forces including for new missions, this concept will facilitate the mounting of NATO contingency operations, the use of separable but not separate military capabilities in operations led by the Western European Union (WEU) and the participation of nations outside the Alliance in operations such as IFOR.'[7]

Whether WEU-led CJTF operations will actually succeed remains to be seen. Potentially serious obstacles include the division among Western European states and their lukewarm commitment to the appropriate military reforms, and the likely hesitation, for political reasons, to lending assets for CJTF missions.[8] In order to adapt the Alliance's capability to its new role and missions, the NAC defined three fundamental objectives: to ensure NATO's military effectiveness in the changing security environment; to preserve the transatlantic link; and to develop the ESDI within the Alliance. The ESDI would be based on an 'elaboration of appropriate multinational European command arrangements within NATO, consistent with and taking full advantage of the CJTF concept, able to prepare, support, command and conduct the WEU-led operations'. This implies 'double-hatting' appropriate personnel within the NATO command structure to perform these dual functions. In fact, the concept of subsidiarity has been established as a cornerstone of European integration.[9] The general formulations and detailed solutions agreed in Berlin ended a significant phase of internal NATO discussion on the future role of the US in the Alliance and on the military and financial commitment of the European allies.

Three aspects of NATO's adaptation

The conceptual thinking reflected in NATO documents in 1996 was aimed at the rapid constitution of a militarily coherent and effective European force within the Alliance.[10] However, many questions remain unaddressed. Detailed planning will be needed to identify and free NATO assets for use by the WEU, including for NATO monitoring of their use. The implementation of the CJTF concept is seen as the first and essential element of the Alliance's adaptation.[11] Meeting in Ostend on 19 November 1996, WEU Ministers agreed that it would be valuable for the WEU to become actively involved in NATO's defence planning and expressed their readiness to participate. Participation by all European NATO members in WEU-led operations (using NATO assets and capabilities) would be decisive for the development of the ESDI.

The second aspect of NATO's adaptation to the new security require-ments is seen in new roles and missions, such as Operation Joint Endeavour in Bosnia-Herzegovina. IFOR brought NATO together with 17 non-NATO countries from Europe, North Africa, the Middle East and Asia, including 12 participants in the Partnership for Peace (PfP) and the North Atlantic Cooperation Council (NACC). The activities of IFOR during 1996 resulted in the successful separation of the former warring factions and in their demobilisation and confinement to cantonments. In the broader perspective, they are an example of cooperative multinational interventionism in Europe.

The third important aspect of NATO's adaptation to the new environment is an intensified effort to address the potential proliferation of nuclear, biological and chemical (NBC) weapons. The NAC defence ministers reaffirmed in Brussels in December 1996 that defence planning should guard against the risks posed by the possible use of NBC weapons and their means of delivery[12] and committed themselves to develop policies based on the Guiding Principles of the Senior Defence Group on Proliferation (DGP).

NATO Enlargement and cooperation with Russia

The ultimate enlargement of the NATO Alliance and the institutionalisation of relations between NATO and Russia are two longer-term components of the process aimed at establishing a non-exclusive security order in Europe. If Central European countries bordering on the former Soviet Union enter the Alliance, the internal transformation and reformulation of its mandate will accelerate. The decisions on enlargement require some agreement with Russia on a formula for cooperation in order to neutralise fears that this process might lead to a new division in Europe and to Russia's isolation.

In his speech in Detroit in October 1996, President Clinton declared that NATO remains 'the bedrock of our common security'[13] and that it can and should do for Central and Eastern Europe what it did in the past for the Western part of Europe: prevent a return to local rivalries, strengthen democracy against future threats, and create conditions for economic and social prosperity. The end-of-year Communiqué by the North Atlantic Council in Brussels recommended that a summit be held in Madrid in July 1997 to invite 'one or more of the countries which have expressed interest in joining the Alliance to begin accession negotiations.'[14] It is anticipated that by 1999, at NATO's fiftieth anniversary and ten years after the fall of the Berlin Wall, the first group of countries invited should be fully-fledged NATO members. In response to Russian objections and reservations, assurances were given that NATO enlargement would not require a change in the current nuclear posture:

> 'NATO countries have no intention, no plan and no reason to deploy nuclear weapons on the territory of new members nor any need to change any aspect of NATO's nuclear posture or nuclear policy—and we do not foresee any future need to do so.'[15]

To avoid criticism that the enlargement of NATO would introduce new lines of division into Europe, the ministers pledged that the Alliance would remain open to accession by additional members in accordance with Article Ten of the North Atlantic Treaty. Certain American criticisms (significantly, revealing a preference for Russian interests *vis-à-vis* those of the Central Europeans and a fear of a fundamental change which might dilute NATO and ultimately destabilise Central and Eastern Europe[16]) were addressed in 1996 with a pledge to slow enlargement, limit newcomers and differentiate between new commitments.

In Russia, the issue of NATO enlargement featured significantly in the 1996 presidential election, but a certain shift in Russia's standpoint could be discerned thereafter. The absolute opposition to NATO's expansion into the Baltic states[17] can be interpreted as Russia reconciling itself to the possibility of a limited group of Central European states being admitted to the Alliance. After the election, Yeltsin demanded a charter governing relations between NATO and Russia be signed prior to a decision on enlargement.[18] An outline Russia-NATO agreement was submitted, calling for a fundamental transformation of NATO doctrine and strategic-operational planning, and joint decision-making—enshrined in treaty—concerning European security, collaboration in implementing these decisions, and joint responsibility for decisions adopted and the effects of their implementation.[19] Leading Russian politicians discounted signing a document of a 'purely declaratory character'.[20] In response to the statement by Prime Minister Chernomyrdin at the Organisation for Security and Cooperation in Europe (OSCE) Lisbon summit,[21] which although implying agreement to the eastward political extension indicated firm opposition to bringing NATO military infrastructure closer to Russia's frontiers. Vice-President Al Gore declared it essential that 'we work in parallel to build a strong and cooperative NATO-Russian relationship.'[22] The fact that the 1996 NAC session in Brussels did not name admissions testifies to a reluctance to ignore Russia's position. Moreover, a document is being prepared on political and military cooperation between Russia and NATO.[23] Russia considers four options in the event that enlargement neither stops nor slows: (a) a redivision of Europe; (b) the OSCE as a pan-European security order alternative and superior to NATO; (c) Russian partnership with NATO: institutionalisation of Russia-NATO relations aimed at joint decision making and implementation of decisions; and, least likely, (d) NATO membership. Moscow will most likely continue to fluctuate between the first three according to different internal and external factors. Its eventual status and external security will be determined more by its success or failure in implementing domestic reform than in preventing enlargement. This does not mean that NATO can ignore Russia's legitimate security interests.

The meeting of Presidents Clinton and Yeltsin in Helsinki in March 1997 demonstrated that it is possible to accommodate different security interests while maintaining opposing assessments of NATO's impending invitation to one or more Central European countries. In their joint statement on 21 March 1997, they agreed that 'the evolution of security structures should be managed in a way that threatens no state and that advances the goal of building a more stable and integrated Europe.'[24] To minimise the potential consequences of disagreement on the issue of NATO enlargement, they announced an elaboration of a document to establish NATO-Russia cooperation. In this way, while respecting each other's different perceptions of national and regional security interests, both leaders demonstrated their willingness to shape mutual relations on principles of cooperativeness and inclusiveness rather than the deterrence and exclusiveness of the past. Russia's participation in IFOR's mission in Bosnia was a qualitatively new experience. It was also a crucial move in developing NATO-Russia cooperation. The politically binding framework negotiated in the recent Charter stands a chance of furthering broad political cooperation, but closer military teamwork—something like a joint brigade—seems unlikely for the near future. Similarly uncertain are prospects for joint NATO-Russian peacekeeping in the former Soviet Union. Some scepticism is in order in view of Moscow's growing criticism of Western security structures (already made clear in the negative attitude towards the Russian role in IFOR).

Cooperative enlargement of NATO constitutes an essential part of restructuring regional security in Europe, but it certainly cannot be substituted for the broader process. This covers the enlargement of practically all Europe's existing multilateral organisations: the EU, the WEU, the OSCE, the Council of Europe, the Organisation for Economic Cooperation and Development (OECD) and many other subregional structures. It is also worth noting that the admission of new democratic states to European organisations—NATO excepted—is not criticised. The most authoritative and forceful criticisms to be voiced by a Western opponent was expressed by George F. Kennan, who warned that 'expanding the North Atlantic Treaty organisation would be the most fateful error of American policy in the entire post-Cold War era.'[25] This argument rests on the belief that enlargement will lead to Russia's isolation, inflame nationalistic, militaristic and anti-Western tendencies, and be counterproductive to the development of Russian democracy. Here two general reflections come to mind which are overlooked as a rule by opponents of NATO enlargement: the first concerns the motives by which the aspirants are guided in seeking Alliance membership; the second the principle of equal treatment regarding the security interests of the states in the region. The candidate countries are motivated by the self-same considerations and concerns which lead the Alliance's present members within it.

Indivisible international security cannot be identified with equal security. Moreover, the oft-declared principle of equal security does not exist in practice. Great powers, by definition, have a greater ability to ensure their own security independently than do small and medium-size states, which see their admission to multilateral structures as a *sui generis* insurance policy against worst-case scenarios. The security interests of this group of states should be taken into account to the same extent as those of Russia. This applies in equal measure to those small and medium-size states that aspire to NATO membership and those which wish to remain outside the Alliance's structure. Tarja Hallonen and Lena Hjelm-Wallén, respectively foreign ministers of Finland and Sweden, emphatically drew attention to the interrelationship of the subregional, regional and global dimensions of security.[26] A special study recently published by the Swedish Ministry of Foreign Affairs stated:

'It is in Sweden's interest that the EU should strengthen its conflict prevention capability so that crisis management, including military operations, can be avoided as far as possible. It may be noted in this connection that the Common Foreign and Security Policy, which is an essential forum for the design of conflict prevention policy, is less effective than the EU's trade policy . . . The divided structure affects the possibility of effectively implementing decisions on conflict prevention measures that are taken within the framework of the CFSP'.[27]

'Innovative conflict prevention activities in Sweden's could have a demonstrative effect on other subregional arrangements in which the EU is involved . . . The aid given to the Baltic states for promoting security has produced rewarding results. In view of the present threat scenario, consideration should be given to the possibility of this support being channelled mainly to conflict prevention measures, including cooperation between the Baltic states and Russia'.[28]

To this end, various other arrangements are already under way in the Baltic and adjacent areas, such as the Baltic and Polish-Ukrainian peacekeeping units, Polish military cooperation with Germany and Denmark, etc.

All this, however, is still far from exhausting the potential for cooperation. A conclusion of the 1996 SIPRI *Report on a Future Security Agenda for Europe* is that three basic values should be included in the security agenda:

> '...each state must still be responsible for its own security, even if it belongs to an alliance; security problems should be addressed according to the principle of subsidiarity, i.e. where feasible, be dealt with on the subregional or regional level; and there must be solidarity between states with regard to security issues'.[29]

Enlargement of NATO and the EU would overcome the historical tendency for Central Europe to be either a region in which armed conflicts erupt and tend to radiate outward or the point of collision between adversaries from the east and west. The report recommended that more attention should be paid to the content and volume of cooperation between institutions than to their structures.

Assessment

In assessing an organisation's effectiveness, an essential criterion is whether the means at its disposal are adequate to the tasks allotted. These means demonstrate the commitment of states to implementing the declared goals. The fact, for instance, that the OSCE's mandate and tasks remain in blatant disproportion to its means suggests both that (a) the OSCE is a lightly bureaucratic body that makes economic and effective use of its modest budget;[30] and (b) that OSCE member states provide insufficient resources. For example, to observe and monitor elections in a credible and coherent manner, the organisation should be able to cover more than a mere five to ten per cent of polling stations. The OSCE was justifiably criticised for mistakes made in the planning and organisation of the supervision of elections in Albania and Bosnia-Herzegovina; while over 3000 individuals were deployed by the OSCE on election day, including election supervisors and observers, the operation revealed both financial limitations and inadequate staff training. The greatest disappointment, however, stems less from the fact that, despite numerous agreements, the existing security structures continue to operate in a badly-coordinated way and duplicate one another's functions, but that at the principal political meeting of 1996 there was no critical reflection on the fundamental question of why these structures fail to meet existing security threats and challenges effectively.[31]

In search of a Security Model

The main result of the Lisbon OSCE summit of December 1996 was agreement on negotiations in early 1997 aimed at adapting the 1990 Treaty on Conventional Armed Forces in Europe (CFE) to Europe's changing security environment. Another decision was reflected in the Lisbon Declaration on a Common and Comprehensive Security Model for Europe for the 21st Century.[32] Both decisions are seen as aiming to defuse Russian fears of NATO enlargement. The Lisbon Declaration identified the common elements for shaping a cooperative European security system as respect for human rights, fundamental freedoms and the rule of law; the market economy and social justice. This also implies mutual confidence and the peaceful settlement of disputes, and excludes any quest for domination. The new political commitments taken under the Lisbon Security Model Declaration can be summarised as follows:

- to 'act in solidarity' to promote full implementation of the principles and norms adopted in different basic documents of the Helsinki process;[33]
- to consult promptly with a participating state whose security is threatened and to consider 'joint actions that may have to be undertaken in defence of our common values';
- not to support those acting 'in violation of international law against the territorial integrity or political independence of any participating State';
- to attach importance to the security concerns of all participating States 'irrespective of whether they belong to military structures or arrangements'.[34]

The commitments to *act in solidarity* and to consider to undertake *joint actions* constitute a positive response to the challenge addressed to the OSCE to define new principles of solidarity and the right to 'cooperative intervention'.[35]

In the context of the debate on NATO enlargement, the Lisbon Declaration reaffirmed 'the inherent right of each and every participating State to be free to choose or change its security arrangements, including treaties of alliance, as they evolve.' On the other hand, the OSCE states committed themselves not to strengthen their security 'at the expense of the security of other States.' Under the Lisbon Security Model Declaration, participating states are obliged to respect transparency in their actions: their security arrangements should be of 'a public nature, predictable and open, and should correspond to the needs of individual and collective security'. The Heads of State and Government instructed their representatives 'to work energetically on the Security Model' and to report on the progress made to the next Ministerial Council in Copenhagen in December 1997. The recommended agenda in this respect should be focused, for example, on enhancing instruments of joint cooperative action in the event of non-compliance with OSCE commitments; further developing the concepts and principles included in the Lisbon Declaration; and recommending any 'new commitments, structures or arrangements' which would reinforce security in Europe.[36] On the operational level, the OSCE is not prepared or equipped to launch military missions. Even thorough attempts to deploy a multinational peacekeeping force in Nagorno-Karabakh (with intensive efforts including the establishment of a high-level planning group) have failed to bear fruit, in the face of the opposition of the parties concerned. The role of the OSCE is determined in considerable measure by the attitudes of the great powers, which often take advantage of its activities. Consequently, the OSCE operational capabilities are frequently hamstrung by conflicting interests. On the other hand, the organisation is reluctant to legitimise actions not in line with its principles, *vide* Russia's attempts to obtain a mandate to operate on CIS territory on behalf of the international community and with its financial support.

Conclusions

First: Of all the regions in the world, Europe has achieved the highest degree of institutionalised security cooperation. Consequently, the focus is all too often on organisational and procedural matters.[37] The real problems, which call for a common approach, are often relegated to second place.

Second: No single organisation—whether NATO, the WEU, the OSCE or the Council of Europe—can handle the whole European security process. The issue at stake is not so much how to enlarge NATO or the WEU, but how to establish a new efficient security system in Europe which will correspond to the new security environment. The focus should therefore be more on cooperation between security-related institutions than on their structures and procedures.

Third: The enlargement and the internal transformation of Western-rooted institutions, such as the Council of Europe, the OECD, the EU, the WEU and NATO, are often perceived as contradictory—deepening versus widening—and as likely to create new divisions. Rather, they should be seen as a natural process and a part of a larger package that could provide credible safeguards for Russian security interests and give Russia a responsible role in the management of European security.[38] The process of unifying Europe should be based on the acceptance of common democratic values and the building of security networks to prevent conflict and find solutions to both common and private security problems.

Fourth: The existing security structures were formed to respond to the threats which are the least prevalent today. They are intended to ensure the inviolability of borders that are no longer disputed. The reforms under way aim to readjust the security institutions to new tasks: domestic conflict prevention, crisis settlement, peacemaking and the development of the new concept of post-conflict peace building. Furthermore, the hopes placed in regional and subregional organisations with regard to security extend as a rule beyond the territories of their member states.

Fifth: The shaping of a new security system, both globally and regionally, is part of a broader historical process in which neither the powers nor the security organisations have exclusive rights. If the regime of global and international security that is emerging as a result of trial-and-error and recent experience is to adhere to the declared democratic values—the rule of law, pluralistic democracy, respect for human rights and the market economy—it cannot be based on the hegemony of one or several powers.[39] Such a system should give expression to the interdependence of states, where mutual relations are governed by generally accepted principles of international law.

Notes

1. Holst, J. J., 'The new Europe: a view from the North', ed. O. F. Knudsen, *Strategic Analysis and the Management of Power: Johan Jørgen Holst, the Cold*

War and the New Europe (Macmillan, London, 1996), p. 198.

2. Urquhart, B., 'The Future Security Agenda', speech delivered at SIPRI, 3 October. 1996.

3. Peters, I., 'New security challenges and institutional change', ed. I. Peters, *New Security Challenges: The Adaptation of International Institutions: Reforming the UN, NATO, EU and CSCE since 1989* (St. Martin's Press, New York, N.Y., 1996), pp. 11-17.

4. Huntington, S. P., 'The West unique, not universal', *Foreign Affairs*, vol. 75, no. 6 (November/December 1996), p. 43. The article is drawn from his book *The Clash of Civilisations and the Remaking of World Order* (Simon and Schuster, New York, N.Y., 1996).

5. Szabo, S. F., 'The United States and new European security challenges', ed. G. Herolf, *Europe: Creating Security through International Organisation*, Conference Papers 17 (The Swedish War College and the Swedish Institute for International Affairs, Stockholm, 1996), p. 21.

6. NATO Secretary General Javier Solana: 'The new NATO and the European security architecture', speech to the Federation of Austrian Industries, Vienna, 16 January 1997.

7. NATO Final Communiqué, Ministerial Meeting of the North Atlantic Council, Berlin, 3 June 1996, Press Communiqué M-NAC-(96)63, para. 6.

8. For a fuller analysis of WEU activities, see Gordon, P: 'Does the WEU have a role?', *Washington Quarterly*, vol. 20, Winter 1997, pp 125-140.

9. Lenzi, G. S. and Martin, L. (eds), *The European Security Space*, Working papers by the European Strategy Group and the Institute for Security Studies of the Western European Union, (Paris, 1996), p. 1. See also 'The European security and defence identity', *NATO Factsheet*, no. 3 (March 1996).

10. In Berlin it was noted: 'the Alliance will support the development of the ESDI within NATO by conducting at the request of and in coordination with the WEU, military planning and exercises for illustrative WEU missions identified by WEU'. NATO Final Communiqué (note 8), para. 7.

11. The CJTF is being developed primarily for operations in non-Article 5 situations, including operations in which nations outside the Alliance could participate. However, the employment of the CJTF for Article 5 operations is not excluded. NATO Communiqué, Meeting of the North Atlantic Council in Defence Ministers Session held in Brussels on 17 and 18 December 1996, Press Communiqué M-NAC(DM)-3(96), Brussels, 18 December 1996.

12. Carter, A., 'Countering the proliferation risks: adapting the Alliance to the new security environment', *NATO Review*, no. 5 (September 1996), pp. 10-15.

13. White House transcript of Clinton speech in Detroit, 22 October 1996.

14. Final Communiqué, NAC Ministerial Meeting, 9-10 Dec. 1996, Press Comm M-NAC-2(96)165.

15. *Ibid.*

16. It 'could provoke the most severe conflict between Russia and the West since the end of the Cold War'. Steel, R., 'The hard questions', *New Republic*, 25 November 1996, p. 29.

17. A letter from Yeltsin to Clinton, excerpts of which appeared in the Russian press, reads: 'Even a hypothetical possibility of extending NATO's zone of operation to Baltic states is out of the question. Such a perspective is categorically unacceptable to Russia, and any steps in this direction would be assessed as an open challenge to our national security interests, an undermining of the foundations on which European stability rests', *Izvestiya*, 6 July 1996, pp. 1-3.

18. This postulate was put forward by Boris Yeltsin on 28 September 1996 at the end of his meeting with the new Defence Minister of Russia, Igor Rodionov.

19. Having presented his concept in the Duma during the seminar on 'The Future of European Security', Yuriy Baturin concluded: 'The envisaged treaty between Russia and the North Atlantic bloc is not a compensation for the latter's expansion. It is not a means of countervailing NATO enlargement. It is necessary of itself or by itself for the creation of a common European security area'. *Nezavisimaya Gazeta*, 28 November 1996, pp. 1-2.

20. Yevgeniy Primakov's statement of 11 October 1996, ITAR-TASS report, OMRI Daily Digest, no. 198.

21. The Russian Premier stated in Lisbon on 2 Dec.: 'We clearly declare our firm opposition to plans of moving the military infrastructure of the North Atlantic Alliance closer to our territory. The appearance of new lines of division in Europe would lead to a worsening of the geopolitical situation in the world as a whole. Russia has not the veto over enlargement of the Alliance, but neither has anybody a veto over our right to protect our national interests. There is still time and reason to consider where NATO enlargement might lead to'. *Krasnaya Zvezda*, 3 December 1996, p. 3.

22. 'Vice-President Gore praises role of OSCE', Al Gore's speech at OSCE Lisbon summit meeting.

23. 'We welcome the aim to conclude a document which could take the form of

a Charter between NATO and Russia. We believe that our relations with Russia can and should be broader, more intensive and more substantive and that they can and should be placed on a more permanent institutional basis'. The Council in Permanent Session was committed to task the NATO Military Authorities to make proposals 'for the development of closer military relationships with Russia and to identify concrete areas for military cooperation'. NATO Communiqué (note 11).

24. Joint US-Russian Statement released by the White House at the Helsinki Summit, 21 March 1997.

25. Kennan, G. F., 'NATO expansion would be a fateful blunder', *International Herald Tribune*, 6 February 1997, p. 8.

26. 'Europe's security is indivisible. Finland and Sweden reject any proposal for regional security arrangements for the Baltic area that is not based on this self-evident principle. We wish to emphasize the value of continued strong US involvement in the area as well as the sense of responsibility for the Baltic region manifested collectively and individually by EU states'. Hallonen, T. and Hjelm-Wallén, L., 'Working for European security outside the NATO structure', *International Herald Tribune*, 15-16 March 1997, p. 8.

27. *Preventing Violent Conflict.* A Study, Executive Summary and Recommendations published by the Swedish Ministry of Foreign Affairs, (Stockholm, 1997), pp. 27-28.

28. *Ibid.*, pp. 56-57.

29. *A Future Security Agenda for Europe,* Report of the Independent Working Group established by SIPRI, Stockholm, October 1996, p. 11.

30. The OSCE budget for 1996 was initially established at a level of 310.1m Austrian schilling (some $28.3m), and with additional tasks in Bosnia-Herzegovina, the budget was revised and established at the level of 546.1m Austrian schilling ($49.837m).

31. The critical remarks of Flavio Cotti remain in stark dissonance with the tone of self-satisfaction demonstrated by representatives of other international organisations who usually appreciate the activity of their own bureaucratic structures highly. See Declaration of the CIO, Federal Councillor Flavio Cotti, to the OSCE Implementation Meeting, Vienna, 22 November 1996.

32 . OSCE, Lisbon Document 1996, OSCE document DOC.S/1/96, 3 December 1996.

33. That is: the Helsinki Final Act of 1975; the Charter of Paris of 1990; the

Helsinki Summit Decisions of 1992; the Budapest Summit Decisions of 1995, and other CSCE/OSCE documents.

34. Lisbon Document 1996 (note 39).

35. The International Working Group report (note 32), p. 1-12.

36. Lisbon Document 1996 (note 39), paras 6-12.

37. See, e.g., Herolf (note 5), pp. 13-17.

38. Blackwill, R., Horelick, A. and Nunn, S., *Stopping the Decline in US-Russian Relations*, RAND Report P-7986 (RAND Corporation, Santa Monica, Calif., 1996).

39. The concept of a 7-polar world, with 7 hegemons, as envisaged by Johan Galtung ('The United States in the Western Hemisphere and the Middle East-clearly aspiring to be the hegemon's hegemon'), like Samuel Huntington's vision of a 'clash of civilizations', may, the authors' intentions notwithstanding, well become a self-fulfilling prophesy. Galtung, J, 'Geopolitics after the Cold War: an essay in agenda theory', V. De Lima and C. Karagdag (eds), *Peace, Disarmament and Symbiosis in the Asia-Pacific* (Solidaridad Foundation, Quezon City, Philippines,1995), p. 55.

PART I
CHANGING INTERSTATE AND INTER-INSTITUTIONAL RELATIONS IN EUROPE AND NATO
LIEUTENANT GENERAL CARLO JEAN

The Cold War's end profoundly changed the geopolitical contexts in which Europe's institutions—NATO, EU, OSCE and WEU—operate. Not only did the threat disappear, but German unification changed the European equilibrium, the US presence in Europe reduced, and Europe became more 'European', in that its autonomy (theoretically) increased as the influence of the Superpowers waned. Europeans must still adjust their present structures to the new environment. NATO, on the other hand, is already doing so rapidly. The initial euphoria and enthusiasm for pan-European organisations, such as the OSCE and the Council of Europe, was soon to be tempered by wars in the Gulf and the former Yugoslavia, and setbacks to Europe's ambitions closer to home. These induced the Europeans to adopt a more realistic attitude, especially as far as NATO's key role is concerned.

NATO is rapidly undergoing a restructuring process. A decisive step in this direction will be taken at the Madrid summit in July 1997, which will decide on the schedule of NATO's eastward expansion, its relations with Moscow and on internal changes within the Alliance. In order to adjust to the post-bipolar situation, NATO has behaved like a company which has lost its share of the market. With the option of closure and disappearance ruled out, it can either scale down its presence in the same market, diversify its product range, or expand.[1] NATO opted to expand its range (moving into security and stability projection from collective defence)

Lt Gen Carlo Jean is President of the Centro Alti Studi per la Difesa (CASD) in Rome. The opinions expressed in this paper are strictly personal and do not necessarily express the position of the Italian Ministry of Defence.

and to its markets (expanding eastwards, striking up new partnership in the East, and opening a new dialogue with the South). The option of downsizing was rejected as irreconcilable with continued operations. This course would have led to a rapid decline in NATO's central importance and would have determined eventual disappearance by encouraging the United States' isolationism. The changes undertaken have not impaired NATO's efficiency, although the most important reforms—new membership; a Russia Charter; reworking the Partnership for Peace, and the creation of the Atlantic Partnership Council (APC)—are yet to be carried out. This is mainly because Alliance decisions are reached by consent, thus in practice by the United States. As leader, the US plays the role of regional integrator and catalyst. NATO's eastward enlargement will not change this: the US will continue to play a global leading role in Europe. The costs of expansion will only marginally influence NATO planning.[2]

Regarding Europe and its main institutions—the EU and WEU—things are more complex. A full overhaul of EU decision-making is needed, but the costs of change would be very high. This much is proved by the difficulties encountered by the Inter-Governmental Conference (IGC) in the revision of the Maastricht Treaty. Objective difficulties in developing the CFSP and common European defence derive, for instance, from the incongruent memberships of the EU and the WEU, and from the wholly different approaches required by the CFSP and EU's economic policy. The former has been pursued in a constitutional manner which implies new loyalties and majority-based institutions. Economic integration, on the other hand, can be tackled by a functional, piecemeal approach. Moreover, in order to contain the costs of the EU's eastward enlargement, changes will be required in basic areas—the Common Agricultural Policy and structural funding—as well as in EU decision-making, if stalemate is to be avoided and the present levels of integration (the *acquis communautaire*) maintained. Whilst US leadership in NATO is largely accepted, the EU has always been a group of equals, each with its own history, perceptions, interests and culture. In the EU no leader exists; integration has been pursued by taking powers from the larger states and increasing those of the smaller.

29

The subjective difficulties, on the other hand, derive from the differing interests and perceptions of the various member states, from their divergent visions of Europe's future and, concerning security, relations with the US. The 'theological' disputes stirred up by the Maastricht Treaty have since abated. No-one now believes that political and strategic Europe can be built without—let alone against—the US. France's *rapprochement* with NATO, and the CJTF concept, which bridges the NATO-WEU gap, have helped to reduced the divergence between the two approaches. The first of these is British and pragmatic, focusing on objectives, means and concrete utility. The second, sponsored by France and Germany and shared by Italy and Spain, concentrates on institutional and formal aspects, i.e. on the ESDI. The continental EU/WEU states submitted a proposal at the extraordinary IGC session held in Rome in March 1997 (the fortieth anniversary of the Rome Treaty) for a three-stage incorporation of the WEU into the EU.

The term ESDI is deliberately broad, ambiguous and flexible. It attempts to reconcile opposed visions. Moreover, it refers to the formal and symbolic aspects, to the visibility rather than the substance, of a politico-military Europe.[3] However in politics perception (including self-perception) count for as much as reality. The ESDI is also an instrument for building domestic consensus. For France, it is a means to prove to a public opinion increasingly suspicious of EMU that the European construction is actually progressing. For Italy, it is evidence that the country belongs to the European core group. The ESDI offers something for everybody.

But what actually is the ESDI? Apart from its cosmetic value, what is the use of a common European defence when all agree that NATO must remain the key institution for Europe's security and defence? How can ESDI reinforce NATO, or at least not weaken it? What effects will the eastward enlargements of NATO and EU have on ESDI? Since these two processes cannot—unfortunately—be simultaneous, what will happen in the transition period? Can a new, solid basis for NATO-EU/WEU complementarity be developed, since security is an indivisible public good which also benefits those who do not pay for it? What are the different faces of the ESDI shown to the East and towards the South? Only by providing answers to these basic questions can the issues of relations between ESDI and NATO or, more concretely, between Europe and the US, be assessed.

Security and defence tasks for Europe

As its economic integration advances, the EU logically intends to take on responsibilities in foreign policy and defence. This desire is also justified by the decline in superpower influence and from uncertainty on future American policy in Europe. The latter is not a problem for the immediate present, and the US is firmly engaged in Europe. Containment has been replaced under President Clinton by enlargement and engagement. Experience in Bosnia has proved that American leadership is indispensable. However, uncertainty over future US-Russian relations and the greater attention paid in the US to domestic issues and to the Asian-Pacific space create reasonable doubts on the future of US commitment, at least at today's scale. The development of a potential European alternative is therefore quite logical, something which would be to hand in the event of American disengagement and, failing this, could give NATO greater flexibility by creating the scope for autonomous European capabilities.

But opinions diverge regarding how Euro-American relations should be structured. Proposals once raised for a Euro-American Pact and a Transatlantic Free Trade Area (TAFTA) are today no longer discussed and NATO remains the touchstone for Euro-American relations. Washington's perception is thus influential regarding any European initiative affecting defence and security matters. In the days of Truman and Eisenhower, the US pushed for Europe's political and strategic integration. Foster Dulles even threatened to exclude from US military aid European countries refusing to enter the European Defence Community. Matters later changed, especially with the arrival of the doctrine of flexible response, which required greater NATO centralisation. The American attitude towards European integration can be seen to have mirrored confidence in being able to exercise leadership: when Washington felt strong, it promoted European integration; when it felt weak, it has seemed ambivalent. With the Bosnia debacle over, the concept for CJTFs, to be employed under both or either NATO or WEU direction, was approved at the Berlin NATO Ministerial of June 1996. As US Permanent Representative Robert Hunter has remarked,[4] CJTF is probably the most important innovation yet introduced into NATO.

The CFSP and European Defence touch not only on the EU's external relations, above all with the US, but also on internal relations between EU/WEU members. They raise essential questions concerning sovereignty and national prerogatives. The debate is influenced by the fact that, since the end of the Cold War, the meaning of security has dramatically changed. In the past it was practically synonymous with deterrence and defence. It has now become multidimensional—in that hard security has been joined by soft security. Broad security management today places greater value than before on non-military instruments, such as development aid or economic levers as a means of deterrence and compulsion. Opportunities to combine economic and military instruments have increased. Europe's security has also become multi-functional, embracing Operations Other than War (OOTW), conflict prevention, crisis management, post-war reconstruction; war against terrorism and international crime, counter-proliferation and so on. Whilst NATO is optimised for hard security tasks, Europe possesses the means for soft security. Its policy of economic support for, and cooperation with, Eastern European, Middle Eastern and North African countries benefits Atlantic security as a whole. The EU could equally cooperate in implementing the infrastructure plan relating to NATO's eastward enlargement. Finally, European security is now multidirectional, since it relates both to the East and to the South.

At this point, a question arises. Can security and defence cooperation between Europe and the US be based on a distinction between hard (NATO) and soft (EU)? If this were possible, it would render the WEU useless. It could be dissolved,[5] while a civil-economic EU became the interlocutor of a politico-military NATO. A higher NATO-EU body could coordinate. This solution, however, fails for several reasons. First, because of the need for a visible European symbol and for a potentially autonomous European capability should the US and NATO one day no longer be present. Second, such a task-sharing model requires the existence of a Euro-American pact capable of managing broad security or foreign policy in general. Third, a clear distinction between soft and hard security is impractical. Military crisis management, for instance, such as a preventive force deployment, demands the capacity for escalation dominance to be effective. What begins as a Peacekeeping operation may turn into Peace Enforcement and the deployment of large forces may be required to support withdrawal of an aborted mission. It is clearly unacceptable for the US to have a mere support role for interventions mounted by Europeans without its involvement. Therefore, as long Europe needs to be able to resort to US/NATO assets in order to intervene, its strategic autonomy will remain limited. This military dependence on the US[6] will increase with progress in America's information-based Revolution in Military Affairs (RMA), especially in what Luttwak has termed the 'post-heroic' age.[7] Whilst Europe is obliged to cooperate with the US to acquire its autonomy, the US is bound by no such dependence and is free to intervene unilaterally.

Fourth, if the European institutions were not reinforced, it would be difficult to maintain NATO cohesion. Without convergence, including in the CFSP and defence policies, the risk exists of a return to the balance of power logic in Europe—one more open and brutal than seen today. In this respect, the assumption that the role of the European nation-states was destined to be eroded, ceding a constitutionalist approach (needed to define common foreign and security interests) to the economist's functionalist concept has proved ill-founded. The best that Europe can therefore hope to be able to do is organise joint policies out of converging national interests. The ESDI, like the CFSP, may unite policies, but it cannot be a single policy. Flexibility has also undoubtedly become more important than uniformity in the post-Cold War NATO. For instance, during the East-West confrontation there was an obvious need to subordinate WEU membership to membership of NATO. At present this need is reduced, even though the US legitimately demands not to be involved in crises without it exercising leadership.[8] Flexibility makes possible more European autonomy.

Fifth, Europe's military component, embodied in the WEU, may offer interesting complementarities to NATO. For instance, an enlarged WEU (at present comprising 28 Member, Observer, Associated and Partner states) anticipates the Atlantic Partnership Council, which will be also created as a political interface to SHAPE's extremely active Partnership Cooperation Cell (PCC). Sixth, the WEU may be entrusted with the so-called Petersberg missions—possibly making use of a CJTF and thus with a connection to NATO, ensuring American coordination and support if the US decided not to intervene with ground forces but, at the same time, did not oppose the European action.

NATO-WEU cooperation was made easier by France's recent *rapprochement* with the Alliance, which reinforced the WEU's character as European pillar of NATO, as opposed to its role as the EU's armed wing The WEU's reinforcement would increase the overall capabilities of NATO without affecting its cohesion, which depends on American leadership. Only by reinforcing both NATO and the EU can the WEU overcome the limbo to which it has hitherto been relegated. The British proposal to upgrade the WEU Council from Ministerial to Head of State and Government level is aimed at increasing its importance and visibility (beside entrenching its independence from the EU, as London wishes).The WEU has to date been keeping a difficult balance between NATO and the EU and has remained independent from the EU. In the short term, it is important that it remain so.

Obviously, US-European relations can never be fully equal. The EU CFSP will be a 'common' but not a 'single'. It will derive from intergovernmental agreements, accords and mediation. Even though the present cooperation procedures may be improved to make them more incisive and visible, the CFSP will be unable to compete with America's foreign policy, which is based on the decisions of single polity. If the CFSP and Europe's defence were to become potentially independent, and the US found itself facing a Europe capable of saying no, it is only reasonable to suppose that Washington's engagement in NATO would decrease. Therefore, a difficult balance must be struck between two opposing needs—the American guarantee and European autonomy—

which are theoretically irreconcilable and can only be pragmatically coordinated. Although a pragmatic approach may suggest a minimalist vision and therefore a merely 'soft' character for the ESDI and the WEU's independence of EU, the unviability of European integration without an overall project and the fact that, if Europe does not proceed in integration, it may revert to a mere single market or even to a free-trade zone make it advisable to keep all options open, particularly as concerns a EU-WEU merger.

There therefore exist basic dilemmas, stemming from the fact that Europe is more a conglomeration of states in transition than a political entity. Some see it as a Frankenstein monster of miscellaneous parts and marked by a wide gap between reality and wishes. As much has been highlighted by the experience of Bosnia and, more recently, of Albania. If these issues of the nation-state and its sovereignty are not tackled with determination and if a process is not set in motion to provide a more solid basis for European decision-making, the European Union may fragment. Eventually, such a process would also weaken NATO, in that it would bring about dangerous re-nationalisation in Western Europe. Integration is an act of will; it is not Europe's manifest destiny.

Dilemmas for Europe's political and strategic integration

These are the hurdles that the IGC seems unable to overcome, although the debate is less characterised by the ideological or theological fervour it had in and up to 1991. There are several convergence points among EU states,[9] namely:

- all agree on the need for action in defence, because of its external and domestic symbolic value, because such a policy may be kept as an alternative should NATO undergo a crisis or the US disengage in Europe and, lastly, in order to reinforce NATO and help it adjust to future challenges and uncertainties. Nobody still sees it as being against NATO or the US;
- the WEU will continue to seek a balance between its function as NATO's European pillar and its role as the EU's armed wing.

These functions must be made compatible;
- there is a need for both WEU complimentarity with NATO and European use of American assets;
- foreign, security and defence polices will be kept intergovernmental. The Council of Ministers will remain the basic decision-making body, while the roles in this field of the European Parliament and the Commission will remain limited at best;
- multinational European forces (such as the Eurocorps, Eurofor and Euromarfor) are to be promoted along with the creation of multinational forces within NATO, with which they must be complementary and compatible. Moreover, there is a need to improve the WEU's decision-making and strategic-operational capabilities (a number of positive steps have been taken since 1991, the most recent of which concerns the CJTF concept). What is still lacking is political will, as proved once again by the Albanian crisis; all the EU Council of Ministers was able to do was submit the request of the Italian and Albanian governments first to the OCSE and then to the UN.

The dilemmas to be addressed hamper the emergence of a strong, stable and unambiguous European identity as well as institutions and mechanisms enabling foreign and defence policies to converge. At present an *ad hoc* approach, based on 'variable geometry' and thus not furthering a sense of identity, still dominates. Political and strategic integration currently amounts to gestures easily criticised for their practical ineffectiveness. What are these dilemmas?

- The roles of Europe and NATO which cannot be solved by merely sharing missions. Fairer burden-sharing cannot be attained without a corresponding reallocation of responsibilities. This would risk weakening the US leadership role in NATO. The accession of 'neutral' Austria, Sweden and Finland to the EU has further complicated WEU-EU relations, already problematic because of non-WEU member Denmark and neutral Ireland. If NATO enlargement is not accompanied by near-simultaneous EU enlargement, difficulties will intensify.

- British opposition to the EU's acquiring defence tasks and to its absorption of the WEU mean that superficial adjustments only can be contemplated. The UK's opposition derives not only from its preoccupation that Europe's political and strategic autonomy may weaken NATO, but also from its fear that the EU's acquisition of a defence portfolio will boost the supranational EU integration process which it rejects. In fact, London emphasises primarily the EU's economic advantages and gives priority to enlargement over deepening.
- The question of the French and British nuclear forces which, despite all openings on *dissuasion concertée*, remain strictly national assets. Any ESDI which did not include nuclear deterrence would clearly be less than complete, but no debate on nuclear weapons is currently feasible in Germany, Italy or a number of other states, and to hold such a debate might prejudice the future of NATO's sub-strategic deterrent in Europe.
- Given the technical parity of all members, the EU is ill-equipped to develop a single foreign and security policy. The reduction of the CFSP to lowest-common-denominator compromises and reduces Europe's presence on the international scene and impedes the intervention of its more powerful states, paradoxically limiting the very autonomy it is meant to foster. Unlike the UN, the EU possesses no Security Council, nor can any of its members play the leadership role of the US in NATO.[10] To overcome this deadlock, the leading powers could be granted greater weight, either through the creation of a *directoire* or through changes in the voting rules. However, this step could reduce the Union's cohesion, creating tension between the larger and smaller states and between those included in the core or *directoire* and those left outside.
- Closely connected with the above is the balance between national sovereignty and collective efficiency needed to create a common security and defence policy. The price of transferring sovereignty to any international institution is not equal for all states. More powerful states must surrender a larger share of their autonomy, while smaller states conversely acquire the powers to

limit or veto their stronger partners' actions. It is not clear to what extent national parliaments are currently prepared to surrender their prerogatives to European bodies. As it has been put: 'If security is collective, it is not security; and if it is security, it is not collective.'[11] The solutions currently debated—variable speeds and geometry, hard cores, concentric circles, *directoires*—are unsatisfactory in reality. Like EMU, they are liable to lead to fragmentation rather than greater integration.

• Finally, there remain deep discrepancies in interests, outlooks and political culture.[12] Concerning the will to use military force, France and Britain hold similar positions, which differ from those of Germany and Italy. Northern European states tend to leave unrest in Southern Europe to be tackled by their Mediterranean partners. Britain historically looked to the US to contain the latent power of Germany, while France has endeavoured to solve it within Europe, by establishing the closest links to Germany whilst retaining its independence of action. Against this, 'German unification has heightened France's wish that the US remains in Europe as a guarantee of European equilibrium.'[13] Italy is meanwhile paralysed by political and institutional crisis as well as by its deficient political and strategic culture and the paucity of its operational capabilities. Finally, Germany has more reason to feel satisfied, but a reluctant power,[14] whose greatest fear is the creation of an anti-German coalition, its weight and potential can still give rise to protests both when it intervenes unilaterally and when it refuses to become engaged.

It may be asked whether so diverse a mosaic as the EU can possibly express any consistent 'identity'. Europe's imagery rests on myths, and theological abstracts are deemed preferable to practical measures because of their supposedly unifying effect. 'Identity' lends a cosmetic unity to the *Europe des patries,* attachments which no-one wishes to renounce, and strengthens the legitimacy of common rules. In the present situation, these dilemmas and contradictions prevent both the emergence of single policies and an incisive European international presence. They obscure the ESDI, often making it incomprehensible to its own supporters. Since it cannot be an actor on the international scene, Europe chooses to renounce what it can actually achieve: an organising role in the European economic security space within a larger Euro-Atlantic context.[15]   NATO thus remains the main factor of Europe's integration.

NATO's eastward enlargement, which will precede that of the EU, will enhance this function of the Alliance, especially if it includes from the outset Central European countries from the Baltic to the Black Sea. On the other hand, a more selective enlargement may widen the gap between the interests of NATO and EU member states. For instance, any enlargement that excludes Romania is unacceptable to France and Italy (and Turkey, one might add[16]) since it would reawaken fears of a Russian re-entry in the Balkans, the Black Sea, and the Eastern Mediterranean. Other NATO members appear to underestimate this factor. An enlargement confined to Poland, Hungary and the Czech Republic could increase tensions between Northern and Southern Europe. The most limited enlargement of all would cause problems by being perceived as furthering an exclusive 'Weimar triangle' of France, Germany and Poland, recalling for Italy exclusion from both the Contact Group for the former Yugoslavia and the proposed OSCE five-member directory. Meanwhile unresolved is the problem of NATO-European cooperation in the South; here, unlike in Eastern Europe, Europe's and American policies do not converge.[17]   The NATO dialogue and the Middle East/North Africa (MENA) Economic Summit are not completely consistent with the objectives of the Euro-Mediterranean Partnership as envisaged at the Barcelona Conference. Since the region is marked by greater instability than Eastern Europe, NATO-WEU coordination implies greater difficulties. This partly explains the problems which arose on NATO's Southern Command.

The ESDI and the Atlantic Alliance

The ESDI epitomises a desire rather than a reality. It does not endanger NATO cohesion and can be useful for the WEU in both its functions as a European pillar of NATO and as the EU's defence arm. Anti-American fundamentalism has largely disappeared from Europe. France and Spain are re-integrating into NATO's military structures. For Italy too, NATO is a means of connecting the Mediterranean to Central Europe, where there is otherwise a marked tendency to ignore the problems of the South or to propose an unviable division of labour.

The ESDI, too, is a bridge, linking EU and WEU, just as the CJTF concept links WEU and NATO. In time it should increase European's sense of responsibility, leading to more balanced burden sharing in NATO and hindering the decline in defence budgets by maintaining an active European role. The US cannot demand that Europe be simultaneously strong and submissive; in reinforcing the ESDI, it should aim to see it as strong and loyal. Without the political-psychological benefits of the ESDI, it will be impossible to strike a balance between NATO and EU/ WEU—a basic prerequisite for any new Transatlantic pact. Without the ESDI, the US would be forced to commit to Europe more than its defence budget, its domestic and its other global preoccupations permit. In this respect, Washington, but also Brussels and the individual European capitals, should evaluate the various possibilities under debate which could strengthen Europe's role and identity within NATO.

- *Convergence between the EU and the WEU.* Most Europeans, with the conspicuous exception of Great Britain, support a process of progressive convergence. A merger of the two organisations is senseless as long as the WEU has no real operational capabilities and the EU has been unable to develop a more effective CFSP— one less tied to total consensus.
- *The CJTF chain of command.* The criticism that the concept implies subordination of Europe's political and strategic autonomy to the US is unjustified. From a practical point of view, no 'variable geometry' of willing and able European states can conceivably reach such consensus as to enable the Europeans to carry out an intervention opposed by the US. Secondly, the CJTF concept increases European autonomy by providing assets without which no intervention would be possible. However, the CJTF concept—rather like the multinational forces now in fashion—is no magic wand, and adequate mechanisms to assign NATO assets

to the WEU and procedures to solve possible disagreements between the US and Europe during WEU-led interventions have yet to be devised. Europe's fundamental problem, even if the ESDI is confined to Petersberg missions only, is not defining a CJTF chain of command for WEU-led missions; it is rather arriving at a CFSP, without which no military force has a purpose, and equipping itself with suitable bodies for crisis and intervention management at politico-strategic (rather than operational) level.

• *A reinforced CFSP*, which must attribute a larger role to Europe's major powers in order to be effective. Only thus can common interests and policies be defined and the initiatives of the willing and able states be shielded from a paralysing need for unanimity. The Analysis and Forecast Centre planned by the IGC and the greater visibility achieved with a 'Mr CFSP', will initially bring bureaucratic rather than political advantages, but will assist the strengthening of the ESDI. A new Euro-American pact is desirable to shape the necessary cooperation with the US. However, should it fail to be achieved, it would be possible to proceed pragmatically, that is, taking into consideration American policies and interests while defining European policies and interests and *vice versa*.

There need be no competition between the practical approach—defining policies on the basis of Europe's actual capabilities—and the abstract and psychological approach of the ESDI. They are two sides of the same coin. Both are indispensable, and compatible with the necessary cooperation between European institutions and NATO. The first is short-term, the second long-term. Naturally, the present must not be mistaken for the future. For instance, an immediate EU-WEU merger would hamper the WEU's capability to serve as NATO's European pillar.[18] Further ahead, on the other hand, such a merger may reinforce both organisations and increase complementarity in an undefined future security architecture.

Notes

1. Josef Joffe, 'Collective security and the future of Europe—failed dreams and dead ends', *Survival,* Spring 1992, pp 36-50.

2. 'Report to the Congress on the enlargement of the North Atlantic Treaty Organisation'. Bureau of Europe and Canadian Affairs, US Department of State, Washington DC, 24 February, 1997.

3. Philip Zclikow, 'The Masque of Institutions', *Survival*, Spring 1996, pp. 6-12

4. Tom Burkele, 'Make the EU a Defence Alliance? Debate deepens security policy rifts', *International Herald Tribune*, 28 March, 1997.

5. Philip H. Gordon, 'Does the WEU have a role?', *The Washington Quarterly*, Winter 1997, pp. 125-140.

6. Carlo Jean, 'Il quinto fronte: gli strumenti militari dell'egemonia globale', *Limes*, No 4/1996, pp. 137-142.

7. Edward N. Luttwak, 'A post-heroic military policy', *Foreign Affairs*, July-August 1996, pp. 33-44.

8. Karl Kaiser, 'Expanding European security space', in Guido Lenzi and Laurance Martin (eds), *The European Security Space*, working papers by the European Strategy Group and the Institute for Security Studies of WEU, Paris, 1996, pp. 3-5.

9. Nicole Gnesotto, 'Common European defence and transatlantic relations', *Survival*, Spring 1996, pp.19-31.

10. John Mearshimer, 'The false promise of international institutions',*International Security*, Winter 1994-95, pp. 5-49, and id. 'Back to the future: instability in Europe after the Cold War', *International Security*, Winter 1990, pp. 50-56. See also Charles E. Kupehan and Clifford A. Kupehan, 'Concerts, collective security and the future of Europe', *International Security*. Summer 1991, pp. 114-161. And Andrew Butfoy, 'Themes within the collective security idea'.*The Journal of Strategic Studies*, December 1993, pp. 490-510.

11. Josef Joffe, 'Collective security and the future of Europe', *op. cit.*, pp. 35-40.

12. Robin Niblett. 'The European disunion: competing visions of integration', *The Washington Quarterly*, Winter 1997, pp. 91-108. And Steven P. Kramer and Irene Kyriakopoulos, *Trouble in Paradise? Europe in the 21st Century*, (Institute for National Strategic Studies, National Defence University, Washington DC, 1996).

13. Philippe Moreau Defarges, 'De la politique étrangère et de la sécurité commune', *Défense Nationale*. Mars 1997, pp. 81-87. p.86.

14 . Franz Josef Meiers, 'Germany: the reluctant power', *Survival*, Autumn 1995, pp. 82-103.

15. John G. Ruggie, 'Consolidating the European pillar: the key to NATO's

future', *The Washington Quarterly*, Winter 1997, pp. 109-124.

16. Przemyslav Grudzinski and Henryk Szlajfer, 'New Europe and Cold War Temptations', *Central European Issues*, Winter 1995-96, pp.121-132; Umut Arik, 'Turkish Foreign and Security Policies', paper delivered to the Centre on Higher Defence Studies, Rome, 21 January 1997; Michale McGwire, 'NATO Expansion and European Security', Centre for Defence Studies, London, 1997; Gheorghe Tinca,'Romania is willing to join NATO', *NATO Sixteen Nations*, Special Issue, 1996, pp.7-11.

17. Ian O. Lesser, *Future Vision 2010: Mediterranean, Europe and Turkey*, RAND, Santa Monica (CA), 1997; Roberto Aliboni 'Institutionalizing Mediterranean relations: Complementarity and Competition',*Internationale Politik und Gesellschaft* No.3, 1995, pp. 90-99; Leon T. Hadar, 'Meddling in the Middle East? Europe challenges US hegemony in the region', *Mediterranean Quarterly*, Fall 1996, pp. 40-54; Carlo Jean, 'Toward a cooperative security system in the Mediterranean',*Mediterranean Quarterly*, forthcoming.

18 . Philip H. Gordon, 'Europeization of NATO: a convenient myth', *International Herald Tribune*, 7 June, 1996, p. 5.

PART II: EUROPE'S AMBITIONS, CAPABILITIES & SHORTCOMINGS

THE WAY AHEAD - PARTNERSHIP OR COMPETITION?
LOTHAR RÜHL

W hile no European defence policy yet exists, the WEU offers structures and opportunities for such a policy to be developed by all full members linked to NATO. The Brussels Treaty, while not complemented by a military organisation with a joint command and force structure, provides a shell that could be filled with substance: designated military contingents, a staff for joint defence and forces planning, political-administrative committees for a common defence budget, common armaments and standardisation programmes, common regulations on military forces etc. The London and Paris agreements of 1954 revised the treaty in such a way that a common defence policy between the partners was always possible, subject to the will being found—and the options are still open. The Maastricht Treaty creating the EU both foresees a 'common defence policy, which might in time lead to a common defence' as part of the Common Foreign and Security Policy, and casts the WEU as an 'integral part of the development' of the EU for military security and defence. The options enshrined in the 1991 treaty are serious and remain open to use.

The evolution of the North Atlantic Alliance since 1991 holds out a reorganised military cooperation between NATO and its European members, almost all of which are in the WEU. The CJTF concept and the related embryonic organisms offer a framework for joint military operations of NATO and WEU forces, using NATO structures and assets (with

Professor Dr. Lothar Rühl is a fellow of the Research Institute for Political Science & European Affairs at the University of Cologne. He was Secretary of State at the German Ministry of Defence between 1982 and 1989 and has been international correpondent of Die Welt since 1989.

the consent of the NAC and thus the US). A NATO-WEU partnership in the use of military means for international security outside the collective defence of the Alliance could become operational in any non-Article Five contingency, including the active military participation of WEU-associated non-members of NATO. The WEU's Petersberg Declaration of 1992 envisages military operations involving these WEU partner states. While neither the WEU's Petersberg missions nor the CJTF concept relate to the collective defence of the Alliance, collective security and collective defence are logically connected for at least two reasons:

- a NATO defence requirement could ensue as a consequence of international security commitments by allied countries in Europe, if and when a crisis or regional conflict escalated;
- Alliance forces (either European and American), if used for prolonged international security missions outside NATO territory (as in the case of the NATO-led IFOR/SFOR missions since late 1995, or in UNPROFOR, the European Rapid Reaction Force and the Alliance air effort based in Italy since before that date) have several effects on NATO's defence capability. They temporarily reduce forces available for the defence mission, but they offer opportunities to train under crisis conditions which resemble combat situations and indeed often include them. They impact on the defence budgets, on force planning, the force structures and the assets and personnel available. They change the outlook for the military profession, the service conditions of conscripts and the rules for peace-time management and training of personnel. Finally, they modify the organisation of logistics and equipment procurement for the forces, particularly those of ground forces.

These effects are clearly shown in the reforms carried out or envisaged in the armed forces of a number of European states, notably France, Germany and the Netherlands. They have considerable consequences for national force structures, personnel selection, equipment and large-scale training. The cost of participation in international Peace Support Operations is high in all cases, even if it varies in accordance with the ambitions and policies of the countries in question. The options available are both complementary and competitive in budgetary terms, in terms of available forces and reserves for sustainability of operations and force structure such as task forces. Since no European country can afford the complete separation of the Projection/Reaction Forces (available for use in international crisis contingencies) from the Main Defence Forces held for NATO Collective Defence, the investment in the former limits that in the latter. Priorities can be established, but they impose trade-offs and compromises for resource allocation between the different missions and force components.

The enlargement of NATO may increase the requirement for Main Defence Forces and will demand the enhancement of military capabilities for flexible and mobile conventional defence, assuming that enlargement is not to be paid for by a weakening of Allied Command Europe's military coherence and an undermining of NATO's core function of collective defence (as redefined by the North Atlantic Council in the Alliance's New Strategic Concept of November 1991[1]). The security extended to new members could only be made real in a crisis provided that the defence capabilities were kept sufficient for this purpose. This condition also applies to the WEU and the EU. A European defence will have to cover all members of an enlarged EU, irrespective of their relations with NATO. Should the latter be incorporated into the EU in the future as its defence component, they will in any case be bound by the WEU's mutual guarantees.

Suggested approaches

The European allies in NATO and the WEU cannot dissociate themselves from their reasonable collective defence commitments on the Continent in favour of crisis management Peace Support Operations; neither can they reserve their limited resources for the hypothetical eventuality of a large-scale short-notice conflict. The possibility for such an emergency exists, but no threat of military aggression can currently be identified in Europe itself: 'European defence' thus has to be based on the assumption that war in Europe has become a remote risk; one that cannot be met with a ready-tailored military response, but a possibility that must be taken into account all the same.

The problem posed by this dilemma for security and defence planning can only find a European solution within NATO by using the WEU, both as a sub-structure of the Alliance and as an instrument for building standardised and versatile European forces with flexible structures, doctrines and training. This is really nothing new, since, before Europe descended into an East-West potential war of strategic immobility, mutual deterrence and forward defence, national armed forces had to be both versatile and flexible to be useful in a variety of different employments. This was particularly true for the colonial Powers of Western Europe, but it also applied to Austria-Hungary, the Ottoman Empire and Russia. The only notable exceptions to this rule were Germany (on a large scale) and Sweden (on a lesser one). Come 1945, with Europe divided and the USSR controlling the East, Western Europe was protected by US military power and nuclear deterrence through NATO. The strategy offered few flexible options outside limits of the deployment plans for Allied ground forces, above all in Germany. Since the end of this state of affairs in 1990-91, defence in Europe has become again a problem of variations, even if the major threat might still arise in the East, albeit with the geographical base of such a military aggression some 1200 to 1500 km further away. The problem becomes manageable for European forces if these can be structured as multinational alliance forces, either by the WEU within NATO as its European pillar, or by the EU (with or without recourse to the WEU as its defence organisation) as the European Security & Defence Identity (ESDI) within the wider NATO framework. The question of a supposedly independent European defence, without or aside from NATO and the US strategic cover, can be disregarded for the time being, since NATO continues to exist (however differently in the foreseeable future) and US forces are still deployed in Europe. This situation may well change during the two decades that follow the year 2000. In this perspective of eventual change, the EU should prepare itself for increased responsibility in the defence field, basing its approach on integration among Europe's armed forces and cooperation in arms procurement.

Solutions to problem of force design, defence planning and the elaboration of a realistic European defence concept, while still based within the context of NATO and US military participation in collective defence, can only lie in greater cooperation and a division of labour among European partners. This should include a common defence industry and common equipment procurement aiming at standardisation and complete interoperability of all European forces within NATO and the WEU. It must be said that the nature of technological development since the 1980s has not favoured European autonomy in NATO, let alone independent European defence without the central participation of the United States. In fact, at the end of the twentieth century, Europe is more dependent on the US lead concerning defence technology, concepts of military strategy and force design, and for the strategic control of military crisis management (using unique Command, Control & Communications, Intelligence, Surveillance and Reconnaissance assets) than at any time since the immediate post-war period.

This poses three major challenges for the Europeans in security and defence terms, challenges which do not permit priorities or resources to be allocated to one at the expense of others. They are:

- the proliferation of ballistic missiles, including NBC capable;
- the potential threat of terror attacks using weapons of mass destruction at all ranges and operational levels of conflict;
- the potential escalation of conflicts on Europe's peripheries and beyond, and the spill-over dangers to European countries of destabilisation caused by the mass influx of refugees and the possible spread of terrorism.

The Europeans must therefore prepare responsive capabilities in NATO and the WEU (but also in the wider context of the EU), including a deterrent force for rising effectively to the emerging challenges by providing for:

- anti-missile defence with a limited, European, scope to face South and East;
- the means of counter-proliferation;
- anti-terrorist capabilities on a European scale with cooperation between all EU/WEU partner states;

- autonomous European arms control, surveillance of arms exports, and verification of international agreements;
- strategic intelligence and reconnaissance by a European organisation, or at least strengthened cooperation;
- strategic transport and communications resources for the projection of European forces in cases of crisis and conflict.

Technology policy

However, neither an agreed European technological-industrial policy, nor a common concept of a practical 'European defence', defined European interests and requirements reached and found by European means and cooperation, seem yet to be within reach. Such cooperation with the US within NATO remains a necessity if a minimum of compatibility and interoperability between US and European forces is to be preserved and the emerging new technologies are to be exploited on a cost-sharing basis for common NATO assets.

The Europeans have agreed on certain objectives and procedures for technological and industrial cooperation, but these agreements are not sufficient to produce constructive results. The EU has not developed common policies either for armaments, for communications and information technologies, or for the aerospace industry. Compromises reached in other fields were based on the continuous economic expansion of the EC and a growing budget that could be distributed in order to satisfy national interests—this is notably true of agriculture, the only real common policy field to date. Since the European share of the world economy is not expanding and the demands on Europe's budget have failed to be reduced by agreement, there has been little investment in truly European objectives of value for the future. Industries do cooperate across Europe's borders, but competition limits this cooperation and national preoccupations with unemployment limits the interest in industrial mergers. The multinational manufacturers either assemble no more than three or four national elements within the EU or engage American, Japanese or other overseas participation of global interest not necessarily coinciding or even compatible with European objectives. The globalisation of the world economy is likely to further 'de-Europeanise' industrial cooperation. The consequences are obvious and unavoidable:

- the EU must either develop a new technological-industrial policy for the preservation of a sufficient armaments production base and technological development capability, or it will have to rely on transatlantic partnership within the NATO framework. This would mean perpetuating the dreaded 'one-way street' of transatlantic procurement along which the flow runs from America to Europe;
- the industries of France, Germany, Great Britain, Italy, Spain and the Netherlands (and possibly also those of Sweden, Austria and Switzerland) will have to merge or arrive at a division of labour in order to develop, produce and market 'European' products to equip Europe's armed forces. (The Tornado fighter-bomber is a good example of this, as is the Eurofighter 2000. Helicopters are not, and regarding Main Battle Tanks, the outcome must still be in doubt, but these are unlikely to become truly European);
- the export of defence goods will have to be 'Europeanised', both in the sense of sharing export markets for joint production and in allowing partners to export products with multinational components so as to make investments pay. Considering parts of the world at present such as North Africa, the Middle East, Latin America and South-East Asia, it is clear that this issue raises questions of a moral-ethical nature.

The effects of globalisation

Transfers of new technologies to Europe often make necessary cooperation with non-European partners, as do the requirements of NATO standardisation and Allied joint procurement. For example, international aviation and telecommunications, airspace control and shipping depend on global solutions beyond the regulating power and control of European governments and institutions. The trend towards globalisation will therefore reinforce itself as it gains momentum. The enlargement of the EU will work in the same direction. EU-exclusive instances will increasingly become exceptional, even marginal. The scope for a European industrial policy will probably shrink from its present narrow base rather than expand. One can even argue that the time of European solutions is waning if it is not already past— before a European approach was able to unfold. Be this as it may, global approaches and interests are likely to determine Europe's activities to a large extent in the key domains of technology and industrial organisation and production, including defence equipment. Inter-regional exchanges of investment and industrial teamings will likewise work against European exclusivity and the strengthening of either European or national production bases for military equipment. This means that dependence on America will grow. There is a distinct possibility of a renewed period of Europeans shopping in the United States for the most important arms and technologies in the domain of defence.

This will, of course, seriously limit all European projects for autonomy in the armaments field, and thus by extension in international security and related policies. A European authority will have to deal with these problems with overseas partners such as the US and Japan, in the World Trade Organisation (WTO), OECD and bilaterally. European policy will have to be different from a purely free trade approach, yet without necessarily being protectionist. It should be inspired more by European security interests in the largest sense than by purely commercial considerations.

Conclusion

Since it is obvious that Europe cannot simply inherit the national interests of 15 or 25 member states and combine these to form a common European interest as a multinational successor to the nation-state, defence must remain a national prerogative. It is intimately linked with the concept and habits of national sovereignty (as is internal security with the national or regional police and administration of justice, or public finance with the tax-levying fiscal administration). For this reason, the Maastricht Treaty of 1991 does not provide immediately for 'European defence' but limits its perspective to a European defence policy, that could one day result in this. However, this perspective has to be widened if the risk of a return to nationally-based concepts is to be avoided. While the renationalisation of security policy is not a likely prospect at present, defence remains a national responsibility in the sovereign states of NATO and the WEU, and it will remain so for some time to come. The enlargements of NATO, the WEU and the EU may well reinforce the trend towards coalition forces and coalition politics in crisis management within the framework of the CFSP. But most European countries can have no interest in turning back towards the past, since they no longer possess the means to support their own defence by themselves—let alone to make contributions securing sufficient influence in the determination of common security interests, political objectives and crisis management. This is also true for the five largest EU partner states, as was shown by both the Gulf War and the Yugoslav conflicts. There is therefore no long-term alternative in the European interest to political-military integration in the framework of the EU/WEU.

In this way, defence cooperation has to be seen as a political, military-economic and technological necessity. The solution must be integration, even if Europe's armed forces remain collections of national contingents. A single European defence ministry is not yet a conceivable institution. What should be conceivable are European defence, security and armaments agencies under the intergovernmental authority of the European Council within the CFSP framework, and subject to the interference of neither the European Commission nor the European Parliament. Herein lies the opportunity for gradual integration.

Notes
1. Paras. 41-54 in part IV of this document.

PART II
THE CHALLENGE FOR EUROPE
YVES BOYER

T asked with preparing some reflections on the subject of Europe's ambitions and shortcomings, I was struck by the different ways in which the subject could be addressed. One is able to choose from among a selection of score cards. According to the more optimistic record, things are not so bad and Europe is making progress. Instead of this, I have arrived at a moderately pessimistic view of the situation, for the reasons that follow.

First of all, I believe that we suffer from a unsolved problem when we speak of Europe, in that I am not certain that we all have the same 'Europe' in mind. I would say that there are probably three conceptions of Europe which are today in competition. The first of these is a 'supermarket' Europe; to the French, this is the British vision. The triumph of Supermarket Europe would amount to the victory of the unfettered market economics of Ronald Reagan and Margaret Thatcher. There is a second vision of Europe, which I hesitate to call a German Europe, but which in France is sometimes associated with Germany, which sees Europe as Switzerland writ large. In this Europe, the economy functions well and people are content, but the continent remains inward-looking and reluctant to play a role on the world stage. And finally, there is a third vision of Europe which, while acknowledging that the matter is still under some debate in France, I shall term a French vision; it is that of a great-power *Europe puissance*. This is a vision of Europe composed of different countries sharing not a number of objectives, but the *single* ambition of affirming Europe's interests, and of defending them—as much through diplomatic as through economic or monetary means. This brings us quickly to the Euro and the hopes being placed in it as a touchstone of European

Yves Boyer is Deputy Director of the Centre de Recherches et d'Études entre les Stratégies et les Technologies (CREST) at the École Polytechnique in Paris.

construction and a currency capable of standing alongside the Yen and the Dollar. The Euro is thus a means, perhaps the only means, of rebalancing our political and strategic relations with the United States. However, for the time being we are still left with these three European visions, and we continue to hesitate between them.

With these three designs in competition, there is confusion concerning Europe's structures. We are all awaiting the EU's Amsterdam Summit, but can we have confidence that the Inter-Governmental Conference is not going to give birth to a mouse? For every sphere in which progress is being made, there is another where it is judged that we can only advance with a few countries at a time; hence the proposal for flexibility in the form of Reinforced Cooperation. The question of the place of the nation state in this new Europe is coming under examination in the debates about subsidiarity, the role of national parliaments and the weighting of national votes in Community decision-making. These are highly complex problems which are still before us and which go to the very heart of the European project. The extent to which we share a common conception of Europe will naturally have, and has already had, consequences for our management of defence and security.

Europe's shortcomings

Setting aside the institutional questions, I also note that Europe is suffering at the same time from a number of extremely disturbing structural weaknesses. The European dynamic appears to be running out of steam. I shall give two examples, the first of which strikes me as the most worrying. This is the demographic problem. Some general figures will suffice to indicate the nature of this. Excluding Russia, Europe has reached a population of approximately 500 million inhabitants, and this figure will remain constant for the next 20-30 years, with no discernible change. But in the same period let us consider Africa. The population of Africa has *increased* by 500 million since 1950 to reach a figure of 700 million. In 30 years time it will have reached 1.7 thousand million. The same thing is meanwhile happening in Asia, and we will in 30 years be faced by an Asia with a population of four thousand million. Meanwhile

Europe's population is not only stagnating but ageing. To take the example of Germany: the unified Federal Republic today has a population of about 80 million. In thirty years this will have fallen to 70 million, with a steep rise in the proportion of those aged 60 or more, with all the attendant problems of health care and social services and the budgetary pressures that this implies.

With Europe's demographic outlook gloomy, the continent's dynamism and its global influence will both suffer. Its economic energy will be threatened. Granted, the European Union is for the moment the world's premier trading power; nonetheless we see a number of new powers emerging, notably in Asia. This is a matter of official record, as exemplified by the fact that, out of nine states to become new members of the IBRD last year, five were from Asia. In the medium term, that is to say out to 2020-2030, it is clear that Europe is going to suffer from structural handicaps which risk slowing down its progress and impeding its cohesion. The project of a great-power Europe, in particular, is threatened by these structural weaknesses.

I would also say—and I regret that this may apply more to the French than to others, but it is still important to mention this—that we have lost sight of the reasons that have guided the European construction. Europe is still moving forward, but we also need to take note of the rise of forces which are fundamentally anti-European. The Maastricht Treaty was passed in France by a bare majority in 1992, and at the first round of the 1995 presidential elections, over 40 per cent of the voters declared themselves for parties with programmes openly hostile to Europe—at any rate hostile to Supermarket Europe or to a Greater Switzerland. This suggests that if a high proportion of French people are hostile to Europe, these are people who could swiftly become disenchanted with a Europe which fails to make of itself, and of the combined energies of its member states, something which functions properly and offers the hope of real action.

Defence and the military

Moving on to matters of defence, I would also underline a number of shortcomings. The first of these, for reasons as much to with economics as with the end of the Soviet threat, is the sharp decline in Europe's military potential. I will not go into details concerning the shrinking defence budgets and reductions in personnel numbers, but all this erodes the operational capacity of the Europeans to act or react. At the same time we see Europe's defence industry dragging its feet over consolidation, despite paying lip service to the idea, while the urgency is properly understood in the United States and industry is actually getting on with the business of regrouping. I would add that there are structural failings in the defence field which affect the Europeans. Take for example what in the United States is called ISR—Intelligence, Surveillance and Reconnaissance: at the European level, it is true that each state provides a certain number of assets, but even collectively we are still vastly overshadowed by the dominance of the United States, which each year devotes on strategic reconnaissance alone a sum approximately equal to the entire defence budget of the United Kingdom and one-and-a-half times that of Italy. In this area, Europe has been well and truly outpaced. And yet it is precisely these very reconnaissance and surveillance assets that we require in order to be able to affirm the European defence identity and to participate in the analysis of future crises, and ultimately in their management. Europe also suffers from shortcomings when it comes to operational planning. The result is that, outside the NATO system and thus without the presence of the United States, the Europeans are unable to plan among themselves for operations of any magnitude. This too we must regard as a major deficiency.

Looking ahead to the future, and using the same horizon of 2030, it is clear that we are far behind the Americans and the series of studies and programmes they have launched under the banner of the Revolution in Military Affairs. In Europe—in France, Germany, Italy and the United Kingdom—this Revolution in Military Affairs is vaguely understood at the level of the Defence Staffs, but no more than that. I am certain that in Paris you will find very few officers who understand and take an interest in these matters—I cannot speak for other countries, but I would imagine that the situation is broadly similar. Thus, compared to the American dynamic of modernisation and adapting force structures, Europe once again appears to be lagging, and not to be taking the necessary measures to allow us to move forward along the path of modernisation.

To those who argue that the scope for military operations of CJTF-type that the Europeans might envisage mounting on their own is extremely narrow, I am at a loss to understand the basis for this assumption, which seems to me to be wholly unproven. We are constantly being reminded of the Arc of Crisis which stretches across the Mediterranean; it is easy to imagine that within 15 years Africa could be a continent threatened with total destabilisation. Without talking of Zaïre, we have already seen the break-up of a number of states in western Africa. I would also draw your attention to the growing role of criminal gangs in Africa. Taken together with the demographic explosion I alluded to above, we could be faced with the prospect of a continent which is boiling over. As Europeans, could we simply wash our hands of the problem? For a number of reasons, I find this hard to believe.

Linking the NATO renovation to the issue of CJTFs, it strikes me that little consideration has been given to the possibility of CJTF being used by the Americans to draw the Europeans into intervening outside the European area. Certain countries still find this hard to conceive of, but the possibility is likely to arise over time through the CJTF mechanism. This is not in itself a condemnation of the CJTF concept, but it is in part related to what happened at the time of the Gulf War of 1991, which brought to the surface the military problems of harmonising command structures and mechanisms for collective action. CJTF is also, after all, a means of allowing NATO, under American control, to act Out-of-Area. I simply ask whether we are ready for this. I have heard German commentators reiterate that there can be no question of German troops being sent outside Europe, at least without certain guarantees. There appears to be a contradiction which we have yet to resolve.

I thus turn from the technical to the more political aspects of defence, since the Europeanisation of NATO—from my own point of view as a Frenchman—poses at the same time military and political problems. It is clearly a military problem if you consider the studies under way in the French army, in view of its restructuring and the reduction in the number of units. It quickly becomes obvious that this reform makes unavoidable France's military reintegration into NATO because of the number of national assets that have been lost and because reintegration is the only military solution left if one wishes to have a significant share in major military operations. On the other hand, if one considers the political dimension, there is still an essential problem, which is that in France (at least) there is still an attachment to this conception of a *Europe puissance* (something reaffirmed by the President of the Republic and the highest authorities of the state); that is to say, a European power possessing the various attributes of sovereignty, including military. On the other hand we see this wish to reintegrate in an institution created during the Cold War and dominated—objectively speaking—by the US.

Conclusion

There is thus a striking and basic contradiction between the political enterprise, which calls for Europe to affirm itself as a power, as much in military as in monetary matters, and the simultaneous desire to reintegrate into an organisation which remains, whatever one says, controlled by the United States. I cannot predict what will be the outcome of the process begun by the French authorities in December 1995. However, the fact remains that they will doubtless have to persuade large parts of public opinion and of the political class to accept both the Euro—which I remind you is part of a complex trade-off with Germany —and reintegration into NATO. Considering these two imminent challenges of domestic policy, I have no idea how it will be possible to justify both of these at the same time, taking into account the line-up of political forces in France today.

I am concerned that many of the present proposals for the 'new' NATO and for CJTF amount to a series of prescriptions for little or no change: the NATO system should continue in the way it was set out in 1949, and improved in 1950. There will be adjustments at the margins, the force levels have been reduced and the Commands have been transformed, but in essence nothing has changed. If this is the Europe that we intend to build, I seriously forecast trouble in certain European countries. Without wishing to play Cassandra, the results could be disastrous if Europe fails to take a stronger line. In France, particularly, I anticipate objections and changes in course. I would end by recalling the episode of the European Defence Community. Launched in 1950 by a vigorous French initiative, the idea was torpedoed four years later by the National Assembly in Paris.

PART II
EUROPE'S ROLE AND THE CJTF
WILLEM VAN EEKELEN

When I am asked to deal with a subject as ambitious as this, I am reminded of the story of the priest and the bus driver who happen to die at the same moment. Arriving in Heaven, the bus driver is admitted immediately but the priest is held for questioning. He protests that he has devoted his entire life to God, unlike the driver, who has caused only accidents. He is given the reply that his sermons sent his congregations to sleep, but that when the driver was at the wheel all his passengers were praying.

I rather see myself as the bus driver. When President Clinton gave his formal endorsement the CJTF concept at the Brussels summit of 1994, I was one of those who regarded it as a revolution in the relationship between NATO and the WEU. Unfortunately the effects of that revolution have been rather slow to come forward, and to that extent I share the frustrations that are sometimes expressed. But it is as well to remember that at that time the United States appeared to be reducing its commitments all over the world and its willingness to respond to crises in Europe. Under those circumstances it seemed logical that we should develop capabilities for action when the US was less inclined to participate. There has been a major reassessment since then, and American foreign policy has once again become much more activist. For that reason, I have reservations when I hear that CJTF is principally aimed at making NATO more flexible. Certainly in 1994, we concentrated much more on the new possibilities of having NATO resources made available to the WEU or to an *ad hoc* coalition.

That was also the time in which concepts I had always emphasised, of multinational forces and double-hatting, seemed to be coming to fruition.

Dr Willem van Eekelen is a former Netherlands Defence Minister and was Secretary-General of the WEU between 1988 and 1994. He currently sits as a Senator in the States-General.

Yet we were simultaneously faced with the problem that, at political level, our governments were making much (too much, in my view) of the idea of interlocking organisations. I always felt that this was mistaken, because international organisations do not naturally interlock. Each has its own identity and role, and there is very little inclination to hand over responsibility to another body. So a neat division of labour, with one organisation requesting another to do something, is a fallacy. You have, of course, to make certain arrangements, but believing that these will mesh cleanly is a mistake. Certainly, regarding the United Nations and the OSCE, my lesson from that period is that the best that we can expect from the UN Security Council is an enabling resolution calling on member states to take all necessary means, or words to that effect. Or even, as with Dayton, rather less than that, and a simple blessing of arrangements which have already been made. In those terms, I think much more of organisations making offers to the UN, or OSCE for that matter, than awaiting ready-made requests. They will never come.

Following the fall of the Berlin Wall, we in the West made much of the argument that NATO would in future become a more political organisation. I rather doubted that at the time, because it had always been this. But I have since noted with some surprise that NATO is becoming more military. All the current discussions, whether with France, Russia or anybody else, are about military matters: command arrangements, infrastructure, liaison, arms control, and so on. I fear that the real political purpose of the Alliance is getting lost. In this respect I believe that the Bosnian crisis came as a blessing for NATO, because it offered the opportunity to do something concrete and efficient. Today, the enlargement question dominates the agenda to such an extent that little energy remains to pursue other questions.

My third point is that during my period at the WEU, we were never able to have a proper political discussion about our aims. Certainly not with the European Union, because if the relationship between the WEU and NATO is not perfect, it is nonetheless heaven compared to that between the WEU and the EU. I was invited only once to a meeting of the General Affairs Council when they discussed Yugoslavia, and I do not believe that my successor has yet been present there.

Fourth: official thinking on CJTF assumes political agreement among the members of NATO, naturally including those which are members of the WEU. I nonetheless remember that we came very close to a break in November 1994, when Washington decided it was no longer prepared to enforce the arms embargo against all the successor states of the Former Yugoslavia while the Europeans continued to insist on its necessity in order to avoid the dangers of escalation. Fortunately, we managed to avoid total breakdown, but it was a crucial moment. Until then I had always assumed that we could reach political agreement on objectives, even if the willingness or ability to participate in a given operation would vary. Let us hope that this will be the case in future, but events in November 1994 showed that it may not always be. In such a situation, the CJTF idea will not work, since it will not be possible to gain the consent of the North Atlantic Council.

A simple conception

My ideal as Secretary-General of the WEU was, I believed, fairly simple. I wanted the Planning Cell first to define what was needed for the various missions, in particular the Petersberg Missions. Then for it to identify what would be necessary for those missions, and to shop around to find out who would be prepared to participate with the appropriate forces for those missions, at least for planning purposes. Then I believed the Cell should compose force packages, and for those force packages indicate a command arrangement—even at that time, I thought that this might mean a multinational NATO headquarters with a separate department for a mission of this kind— and the appropriate communications, logistics and transport functions. By this stage, it would have become simpler to define what assets were still lacking and where an additional element was needed to complete the operation.

In the event my ideal foundered, primarily because Germany was not prepared to enter into contingency planning. The Germans considered that the whole issue was too sensitive politically, especially in view of the government-*Bundestag* relationship and were not prepared to commit themselves to such specific planning. It was possible to resolve this to a certain extent by using generic scenarios, but still this type of planning is very difficult if countries are not prepared to enter into a certain amount of detail. It is also then very difficult to ask countries to indicate with any certainty the forces which ultimately might become available. Without those indications, it is very difficult to plan for anything. I believe that this will also be one of the major problems in the context of CJTF. Can you really count on forces becoming available for specific situations? Or must planning remain so generic that you are still dependent on political decision-making, something which may be very time-consuming. Germans may protest that their country is ready to act in the NATO framework, but that is unfortunately not the entire solution. What do we do in a situation where the US does not want to participate? I thought in 1994 that CJTF might provide a proper answer to this, but we do not seem to have found it yet.

I have another point to make concerning Germany. I have a feeling that the real problem for Germany is that it still has conscription. I have nothing against conscript-based armed forces; in fact, I wish that we still had them in the Netherlands. But the present organisation of the German military works against the possibility of use being made of it for this kind of intervention operation. Step-by-step that position is changing, but it remains difficult. Without German personnel we may find that we do not have sufficient forces for European operations. Basically, I felt that Bosnia could have been dealt with by Europe, by the WEU, but there was no political will to do so. Only France, the United Kingdom, Benelux and Spain were able to send forces, Italy then being disqualified by UN rules.

Operational and political variables

I am concerned that, as Europeans considering our military role in the future, we are still focusing too much on very large operations. I think that everybody today agrees that it is for NATO to organise such operations. This is also the value of having France back in the Alliance military structure. The role that we need to play as Europeans, whether in crises in Bosnia or Albania or somewhere in Africa, is that played by police in national societies. This role is needed in international society and it is still lacking. The United Nations is not playing it—merely acting, and even then inefficiently once fighting has erupted. We need to pay much greater attention to the sort of preventive deployment seen in the Former Yugoslav Republic of Macedonia. There, with 500 men, the United States and the Nordic countries have done something which is invaluable in preventing escalation. For missions such as these, speed is of the essence. In Albania we were not speedy enough to do something effective, which is to establish islands of stability, from which hopefully an effect will percolate into a wider area. We need to be able to intervene between the combatants when there is a ceasefire, and to be there so rapidly that the violence cannot start again before we have arrived. There are those who respond by warning of the need for escalation dominance. Of course, you have to be prepared to defend yourself and aware that a peacekeeping mission may potentially escalate into a major operation. But the basic role should be stability enforcement, not warfighting. Warfighting we should leave to NATO, and for a very long time to come.

The sort of missions I have referred to are relatively small, and this also is true of the forces they demand. General Joulwan once explained to me that, in the absence of clear planning instructions from the North Atlantic Council, he was planning for a Corps-sized operation in Bosnia of, say, 50 000 men. The headquarters required for this numbered 2000, including 800 people for communications and 400 for general support. This headquarters alone was far bigger than any WEU operation we were mounting; we had 250 police and customs officers on the Danube, and a target figure of 180 in Mostar. For the WEU, thinking on a NATO scale would have been completely inappropriate. Looking back, I believe that we have all made the mistake of exaggerating the need for NATO assets. Because in the majority of situations, certainly when you look at the lesser missions undertaken by the WEU, it has not needed any additional assets at all. It is correct that the Nucleus for a CJTF HQ could come from WEU, but the question that then remains is whether there is a need for NATO assets to organise the operation. Maybe for the real-time intelligence assets, and of course strategic lift, but we will still be left with the problem of how to organise the real-time intelligence if there is not an American element in the WEU headquarters. For our operations in the Adriatic, in the Iraq crisis of 1990, on the Danube and in Mostar, the size of each WEU operation was such that these assets were not needed. Again, in the case of the Bosnian operation, we could get there by rail and road, and the whole question of strategic lift did not arise. As a result, I felt that the headquarters question was really the most important, and this gave rise to misunderstandings and frustration. I insisted that the WEU should not mirror NATO and therefore should not duplicate its headquarters arrangements. But, to my surprise, the fact that WEU did not have a separate command structure was held against it by those who wanted to criticise the organisation. Without these attributes, we were accused of being powerless by the very people who would have accused us of duplication and of risking the internal erosion of the Alliance had we done otherwise. In this area I believe we have still not entirely resolved the paradox. What we lacked then, and still lack, is a sufficient interface between the WEU Council and the Force Commander in the field; I am not persuaded that the arrangements that have been made in the meantime are sufficient.

I think a crucial question, when talking about the European Security and Defence Identity and thus European-led CJTFs, is that of how the WEU should make its political input at NATO. It is not entirely clear where either NATO or France stands on this matter at present. I understand that France has now accepted that NATO is a useful instrument not only for collective defence but also for crisis management, but what does this mean for the European element in NATO? Is it only a military issue? In my view, military problems are always the easiest to solve, since the military, once informed that you wish to see a certain outcome, will make it happen. Or is this also a political question? For my part, I cannot see how you can have a European Security and Defence Identity without it being possible to introduce common European views within the Alliance. Whether those views are developed within the EU's Common Foreign and Security Policy or the WEU is not too important at present. In the long run, I believe that the CFSP will probably have to provide the background for European decisions. I don't think the need is for a 100 per cent *common* foreign and security policy—that will never happen—but, as we saw in the Kuwait crisis and in Bosnia after some difficulty, it should be possible to frame a common attitude on a very specific issue that has been well analysed and prepared in advance. This should then be maintained as a basis for common action. What is most important is that this should be introduced into NATO consultations, and naturally in a way acceptable to the United States.

Some may recall that I used constantly to ask what was needed to keep the US interested in Europe and that my answer was that we must organise ourselves better, because if we Europeans continued to act in dispersed order, it was unlikely that the US would continue to bother itself with our security. To a certain extent I already see the fruit of that. The Americans are again much more interested in remaining a player in Europe, and we scarcely hear calls for greater burden-sharing any more. This is a fairly fundamental change from the days of the Cold War, when the Americans made the major contribution. I think that the cost of that American presence is bearable today. The issue is not whether the Americans need to keep 100 000 soldiers in Europe. I would have been perfectly happy with 70 000 four years ago.

However, the most vital question of all, as I saw it in 1994 and still see it today, is whether the United States will participate. 'Ask NATO First' is not really the central question, which is this: are there situations in which the United States may be with us politically, but not in terms of substantial force contributions? I disregard the presence of certain American headquarters staff added to a headquarters that is European-led. Are such situations actually likely to arise today, as it seemed in 1994? As I have pointed out earlier, the United States is now in a more activist period and I am not persuaded whether the scope for CJTF is really very great. Already we have seen the types of operation which WEU or an *ad hoc* coalition might contemplate, for which NATO assets are not strictly needed. Alternatively, a major operation would be so large that the Europeans would not wish to start without proper American support and participation. What is this area in the middle, for which the CJTF concept might really be useful? It is not clear to me, and I believe that this needs to be clarified.

Conclusion: looking ahead

Looking ahead, what can we expect to emerge from the Amsterdam summit? Two things, I hope. First, that the notion of Flexibility will be introduced into the European Treaty. To my mind, this is essential if a European Union expanding to 20 or 25 members is to have any capacity to act at all. Second, I should also hope to see the Petersberg missions incorporated into the Treaty. These must include Peace Enforcement, without which the change would be no more than cosmetic. This development will pose a major question mark over the political role of the WEU, because if the major missions of the WEU are in the Treaty, the CFSP will become the main forum for dealing with matters of that kind. Of course, one advantage would be that the five present WEU Observers are at last fully involved in those Petersberg missions, and I think that that would be no mean achievement. Today, there is inherent friction in having 15 states in the CFSP and only ten as Full Members in the WEU, and the present arrangements with the Observers are not really up to filling that gap. I think the WEU's Planning Cell should be maintained and its Security Studies Institute also, but I am less sure about the role of the Council. The new role of the CFSP will beg new requirements regarding a channel between the CFSP and NATO, so that the flow chart (which is apparently developing well) may thus have to be reviewed sooner rather than later.

I end with the observation that CJTF was a great idea in 1994, but that it took far too long to develop. I shall conclude with two warnings. In the first place, what strikes me—and I say this as the one-time bus driver— is the emergence of hidden agendas, all over the place. They lead to enormous ambiguities, with countries saying different things in the CFSP, the WEU, NATO and the UN Security Council. If this continues there will be recriminations all round, but in the end the willingness of our populations to contribute to defence will suffer. I don't think that our people will be prepared to pay for forces if it is clear that they will never be used, and if governments continue to shift blame around and duck responsibilities.

Closely connected with this is the question of political will. I have been quoted as saying that we, as Europeans, ought to have been able to manage Bosnia. We *should* have been able to muster some 40 000-60 000 men. However, the matter did not arise because there was no will to take on that responsibility, even allowing for some countries being less able than others to rise to this. I fear that as long as that political will does not emerge, not only will things not work in Europe, but they will not work in NATO either.

THE US AND EUROPE: A PARTING OF THE WAYS OR NEW COMMITMENTS?
ROBERT E. HUNTER

We have joint councils of NATO and the WEU. At WEU there is a term for everybody. There are Members and Observers and various flavours of Associates. Unfortunately, when we go into the WEU Council Chamber, there is no category for Americans. So, when we first went there, instead of having a nice, finely-etched plastic sign with the name United States, they had to write something up on cardboard. I have thought that maybe WEU should have a category called Friends of the Western European Union. That would surely encompass my country.

Two questions are being posed here. First is the overall question of CJTF as 'A Lifeline for A European Defence Policy'—*question mark*. Then comes 'The US and Europe, A Parting of the Ways or New Commitments'—*question mark*. Let me advance a third question: why are we still questioning the role of the United States—*question mark*. This is what we would call in my country A Settled Issue. The United States is here, and we are here to stay for as long as our friends and our Allies here in Europe want us to stay. We did go through an era of doubt and questioning after the Cold War. That itself is probably a source of strength: the engagement we have here is not a product of habit, but a product of cold-blooded analysis. The United States is a European power. I would have thought that that would have become clear to us, as well as to our European friends, after three engagements here in this century, and we are now embarked upon the fourth. We obviously do it for political, economic, moral, strategic, and military reasons, and it is a bipartisan commitment. The transformation of the American role here was begun by President Bush in the wake of the Cold War, and it was carried on by President Bill Clinton. I am pleased to say that, as we go

---

Ambassador Robert Hunter is US Permanent Representative to NATO.

through the great debates of this year and the year to come about the future of NATO and its enlargement—expansion, opening, whichever word one chooses to use—this is not dividing along party lines. There are some serious issues at stake, and there will be as we go through the process of ensuring the two-thirds vote in the Senate that is needed for new members to be taken in. But the divisions that we have are not along party lines, and in fact the US commitment on this is deeply bipartisan.

I should point out, of course, that at first the re-definition of the American role and commitment was not fundamentally about the defence efforts of Europeans themselves, not about the European Union, and not about WEU. But as time went by after the Cold War, we in the United States did realise that, first, history had not come to an end. If anything, in a number of countries in Central Europe and beyond, there was a rebirth of history. In fact, we now find ourselves at NATO dealing with the after-effects of not one twentieth-century European war, but of all three of them: the First World War, the Second World War, and the Cold War. We are trying to deal with the consequences of all three at once. We have realised in the United States that security in Europe does matter. It matters to us, and it is a priority that we will pursue regardless of what other distractions there may be elsewhere in the world. A question was posed a few years ago about the choice to be made by the United States between Europe and Asia. That was never a real choice, and we have answered it conclusively. The answer is both.

The second proposition that we have come to realise is that, after a good deal of experimentation, after recognising the importance of other institutions—including OSCE, the European Union, WEU, and the Council of Europe—the institution most important to us for dealing with security issues in Europe for the foreseeable future is, once again, NATO. Certainly NATO is the institution in which the United States will define its own engagement in European security. We will do this through NATO more than any other institution, including others like OSCE, to which we also belong.

The third recognition in America, and, I think, in most if not all Alliance member states, is that NATO is effective when the United States is prepared to be engaged, and indeed, when the United States, with the willingness of its allies, is prepared to lead. I am pleased to say that my country is prepared to lead. It was under President Bush, and it is under President Clinton, as we move forward. We saw President Clinton's leadership in January 1994 at the Brussels Summit, which launched the three basic adaptations of the NATO Alliance: the internal structures, about which I shall say more; outreach to the East; and the embarking on new missions, which included the invention at that time of the Combined Joint Task Forces or CJTFs. The purpose of these is, let me underscore, first and foremost to increase the capacity of NATO to operate. From the US perspective, CJTFs are most important with regard to what they enable the Atlantic Alliance to do. Thus we have also seen the engagement of a NATO-led operation in Bosnia, including all 16 of the NATO Allies. You may bring me up short and ask about Iceland, which has no forces. But it has sent some staff officers, two doctors and a nurse. Fourteen members of the Partnership for Peace have also sent forces, including Russia.

NATO's agenda

We will also move this summer, on 8-9 July in Madrid, to advance seven major activities of NATO's future. I think you know them well. In the first place, we will invite a limited number of countries, from among the 12 which have formally applied, to open accession negotiations with us. Following the conclusion of these negotiations, the 16 parliaments will begin discussions to take these countries into NATO. These are, after all, commitments of nations, not just of governments.

Second, the door to NATO membership will remain open. My country's position is quite clear. From our perspective in the United States, the door to NATO membership will remain open so long as there are European countries ready and willing to bear the burdens and the responsibilities of NATO membership.

Third, we will expand, augment, and deepen the Partnership for Peace— perhaps the most successful venture among NATO's activities.

Fourth, we will inaugurate some time this spring a Euro-Atlantic Partnership Council to replace the old North Atlantic Cooperation Council, to give members of PfP a major share in determining the future of that effort.

Fifth, if matters proceed, we will see the conclusion of a document—a charter, we call it—between NATO and Russia, possibly in Paris on 27 May, as the Russian President has predicted.

Sixth, we will conclude a parallel relationship—similar but not identical—between NATO and Ukraine, recognising that country's special significance in the heartland of Europe.

Finally, we will carry out further work on what we call the Long Term Study to refine, advance, modernise, and make more flexible the NATO command structure. Among other things, we will be dropping from 65 headquarters to about 22 or 23.

In addition to this very daunting agenda, there is also what I would call the Eighth Imperative. The Eighth Imperative is to move forward with the relationship that we at NATO are building with the Western European Union, in support of a European Security and Defence Identity (ESDI). It has deep value. Indeed, from our perspective, as we look to our engagement here, this is something we consider at this point to be indispensable. There has been the long-standing American concern for the evolution of the European Union, which we have supported since the Rome Treaty over 40 years ago.

The US and the ESDI

During the Cold War, however, the United States was ambivalent about what today we call the ESDI. We wanted to have a strong European contribution to Allied defence. We wanted to see this started and nurtured but, at the same time, we wished our European allies very much to follow closely the lead of the United States. We believed that, for what we saw then to be good and sufficient reason, there needed to be a single centre of decision-making—namely, through NATO and with US leadership—

for managing the critical relationship with the Soviet Union, and especially the nuclear dimensions of that relationship. American policy with regard to the ESDI and the WEU has changed fundamentally since that time. It happened formally at the Summit in Brussels in January 1994, again, for good and sufficient reason. There was the end of the nuclear relationship with the Soviet Union, the end of the Warsaw Pact, and, indeed, the end of the Soviet Union itself. In fact, by using the same methodology, the United States came to the opposite conclusion and became a wholehearted supporter of both the WEU and the ESDI.

Why this change of heart? In the first place, there is the role of the European Union in the institutional framework of Europe. Second, there is our concern to see continued support for European engagement in the common defence effort, a point to which I shall return later as one of the greatest challenges I think we now face. This is a critical part of responsibility-sharing within the Alliance. This is not the same as the old burden-sharing, which was a matter of trying to shift costs. It is rather to have a significant European effort within the overall framework, including a good deal of added European decision-making along the way. This contribution—this continued contribution—will be critical for us in our relationship with the United States Congress. In addition, a strong WEU, a strong ESDI, is a supplement to other institutions in ensuring the continuation of full Western integration. To put it more directly, this is part of the full engagement of Germany and its relationships with others in a broader institutional framework, something which has had the support of all German governments since the Second World War. Furthermore, there is a US desire to see the European Union and WEU— certainly the former—engaged actively in reaching out to the East. I should say at this point that what NATO is doing we see very much as attempting to complete the work of the Marshall Plan 50 years ago — work which was stopped at the Inner-German Border by Marshal Stalin. In one of these rare instances, we have a chance to revisit history and to complete that work.

Quite obviously, what NATO does in becoming engaged in Central Europe and with Russia will count for little in the fullness of time if the

European Union and ancillary institutions are not also able to do what they are bound to do. I am not trying to create a linkage between NATO enlargement and EU enlargement, but simply to say that, if the two efforts do not complement one another and proceed in parallel, I doubt whether either will succeed very well. Finally, we Americans are going to be here; we believe that we will be fully engaged in all important European security problems. However, there will be people in Europe who are sceptical of that assertion, just as there were sceptics under more demanding circumstances at the time of the so-called de-coupling crises of the Cold War. Thus it is useful to have the WEU as an insurance policy in case the United States does not choose to be engaged in all areas.

As a result of this reasoning, we proposed a deal at the 1994 Brussels Summit. In exchange for our European Allies not attempting through the ESDI to duplicate a set of resources which, frankly, none of the European countries were going to build anyway—this is a matter of political will and resources—we declared we would be prepared to take the lead in gaining agreement at NATO for direct support of the WEU, based upon the concept of 'separable but not separate' forces and assets. We also proposed at that time that the CJTFs could also be a major instrument in making available to the WEU, under appropriate circumstances, assets that are uniquely available to NATO. We are gratified that our European friends and Allies responded to this American offer; in particular, in December 1995, that the government of President Jacques Chirac took the fundamental decision—I think a politically courageous decision—to respond in kind. It agreed with the proposition that the ESDI should be built within NATO, not outside it and in competition with it; that it should be supportive of the transatlantic link rather than a rival to it; that there should be one NATO, not one structure for so-called Article Five operations and one for other operations; and that, indeed, the role of the Supreme Allied Commander, Europe (SACEUR)—which had for a number of years been in question—should be reaffirmed, and that role recognised and ratified.

The progress made was, I think, quite startling. Within a week, the French Ambassador and I were able to complete the work at NATO that led to the opening of CJTFs to the WEU, and that work has proceeded as a more or less technical exercise ever since. At Berlin and Brussels last June, we at NATO agreed on a number of activities, which we have gone forward to implement. In the first place, the WEU has provided NATO with some six generic scenarios of operations that the WEU might want to undertake. We have now completed the planning on two of those scenarios, and will shortly transmit the results of this planning to the WEU, now that the question of the role of WEU Associate Members in operations using NATO assets has been resolved, through French leadership in the Presidency of the WEU. These plans, incidentally, while done at NATO, are a unique set. They could be implemented by the WEU, but they could also be implemented by NATO.

CJTF mechanisms

We will then proceed to identify officers within the NATO structure who will have their regular NATO responsibilities, but who also could be separated out to work directly for the WEU. Let me note that if, in this identification—either directly or through a CJTF—that includes American officers, they would, indeed, also transfer to the WEU, if overall agreement is reached on a particular operation. We at NATO are also prepared to transfer other assets. We have now worked out the terms of reference for the Deputy Supreme Allied Commander Europe (DSACEUR). Not only will he be in charge of planning operations under the authority of SACEUR, but, if indeed there is a transfer of NATO assets to the WEU, he could become the WEU strategic commander. I say *could* because if a minor operation is undertaken, the WEU might not want to use a four-star general, but someone junior.

We have also worked out the mechanisms whereby NATO assets would be released to the WEU. In fact, I would say the work that would be required to make this real is about 99 per cent done. This includes, in the process, a greater Europeanisation of the NATO command structure and an increased effort to show visibility to the European components thereof. Let me point out, however, that in the process of making this relationship effective, there are a number of key principles that we think need to be recognised.

In the first place—and this is agreed by all—there is the need to preserve the NATO chain of command and its integrity. It will be possible to separate out forces and other assets to be used by the WEU—including, in parallel, assets unique to the United States—but it must be done in a way that NATO can continue to work. It must also be done in a way that, if there were some urgent need for NATO to reclaim these assets for its own use, that can happen.

Second, there must be a preservation of the linkage across the Atlantic. Third, there must be preservation of the concept of one NATO, not a bifurcation. Fourth, we wish to minimise duplication of assets, whether in terms of forces, officers, or the like. Fifth, we have, as Americans, argued that if there is something of true significance in Europe requiring military action, it is very likely that the United States will want to be engaged. We have asked our friends at the WEU to ask NATO first if they are contemplating an operation. If the United States and the WEU Associate Members (or Denmark, as an Observer) choose not to be engaged, then the WEU will have our blessing to proceed on its own with the use of NATO assets. Let me underscore that the WEU, if it does not call upon NATO assets, is free to undertake its own activities at any time.

This question of asking NATO first relates in part to responsibility-sharing. It is not a matter of trying to keep the WEU from doing anything. Let me state again: the WEU is sovereign. Its ten countries can do anything they wish without let or hindrance—we will have nothing to say about it. Rather, it is a question of whether there is a desire for the WEU to use NATO assets. And if the US wants to participate, we would like NATO to be asked if it wants to take command of the operation, and to run it. If indeed it were something that we would like to be involved in, and our European friends said: 'Butt out, we don't want you,' I suspect we would reply, 'Fine, you're on your own.' The irony is that, for 48 years now, the problem has been seen the other way—that somehow the US would not want to be engaged. I am saying: please give us a chance to be part if we wish to.

Tests ahead

In our view, the question of the WEU-NATO relationship is less about who will actually undertake an operation than about the overall contribution to security. We do not, as Americans, see the test of the WEU's effectiveness as being whether or to what extent it actually engages in military operations. The test is rather the activity of creating the ESDI, the willingness to use it, and the preparations to undertake those matters which could come before it—preparations which, in themselves, could prove to be the WEU's most important contribution to European security. Still to be tested, I believe, are a number of propositions. First is the willpower of the ten WEU countries to move forward to make this institutional framework effective. Second is the level of defence commitment that all of our countries in the Western Alliance, including my country but certainly our European friends, are prepared to undertake. We face a particular challenge now: we are designing an architecture for the future with which we believe we will be able to work effectively, but we could find that some or all countries are unwilling to make the contributions in resources that are required for us to have an effective security structure. We must at the same time collectively avoid a hollowing out of our different alliances— including a requirement which I have not addressed: the relationship between the defence industries of Europe and North America that today does not exist to the degree necessary to sustain public and industrial support for our mutual security in the future.

We will also be tested—not just the WEU, but all of us—by our ability to adapt to new circumstances. I am not sure that any of us, institutionally speaking, can be proud of the manner in which we dealt with the recent and ongoing crisis in Albania. I think it is a tribute to our Italian friends and allies that they took the lead in these particular circumstances. I suspect, however, that for WEU this was a missed opportunity. I do not know of a single member of the Alliance that would be prepared to get into another situation like that of UNPROFOR. There are a number of reasons that events in Bosnia took the course they did, and I think we have all learned a lot from that. If we could run the newsreel back to about

1992, I suspect we could, individually and collectively, give matters in the Former Yugoslavia a very different outcome. I regret that the people of Bosnia and some others have suffered mightily during our learning experience. But I hope that we have all learned those lessons adequately. I have outlined a few propositions. We believe, at NATO and I think also at the WEU, that we have designed the requirements for the defence architecture of the future. We now have to make it work.

PART III
NATO'S STRUCTURAL REFORM AND THE ESDI
MARC BENTINCK

From its title, this study is focused on Combined Joint Task Forces (CJTFs), not only as such but also as a lifeline for a European Defence Policy. The use of this term conveys a sense of urgency, if not outright drama, which might not be shared by everybody. At the same time the lifeline idea does bring into stark relief the plausible notion that a credible European defence policy somehow needs to be kickstarted, if you will allow this rather colloquial motoring expression. As we delve into the CJTF concept, we might indeed discover that this has among its many qualities the capacity to kickstart, or at least stimulate, the development of what is generally called the European Security and Defence Identity. As a further contribution to considerations on this matter, I will endeavour to present an overview of where matters stand on CJTF from the perspective of NATO's International Staff. I shall concentrate on those elements which appear directly relevant to the Alliance's commitment to support the building of the ESDI.

The broad chronological context

One should first recall the broader context of NATO's internal adaptation. I feel obliged to refer to this since the work on the implementation of the CJTF concept is intimately bound up with a political-military process triggered by the strategic earthquake at the end of the 1980s. In fact, had the Allies not early on recognised and acted upon the need to respond to the landmark events of 1989-90, work on CJTF would not have progressed to the point we are at now. Starting with the Summits of London (1990) and Rome (1991), the Alliance set itself the task of adapting its procedures and structures to the new strategic environment.

Marc Bentinck is Head of Defence Policy in NATO's Defence Planning & Operations Division

From the outset this adaptation was also meant to enable the European Allies to shoulder a greater responsibility for both the common defence and NATO's new missions, while avoiding costly duplication of forces.

As set out in the Alliance's new Strategic Concept of 1991, the security challenges and risks to Allied security that remain are multi-faceted and multi-directional, therefore hard to predict and assess. The Alliance's ability to deal with the many possible contingencies arising from today's instabilities call for a new flexibility in the generation and deployment at short notice of military forces. This new flexibility was found in a concept that builds on NATO's well-established practice of multinational, multi-service operations: a deployable multinational formation generated and tailored for specific contingency operations. These operations could be of either Article Five or non-Article Five nature, possibly involving humanitarian relief, peacekeeping or peace enforcement, but also collective defence.

Launched in 1993, the CJTF concept was endorsed at the Brussels Summit of January 1994. On this occasion the Alliance's Heads of State and Government directed that the further development of the concept should also reflect the readiness to make NATO assets available, on the basis of consultations with the North Atlantic Council, for WEU operations. Furthermore, they linked the further development of the CJTF concept to practical political-military cooperation with non-NATO nations in the context of the Partnership for Peace.

In the period that followed the Brussels Summit, the development of the CJTF concept came to constitute the main practical dimension of the Alliance commitment to support the building of the ESDI. The notion of CJTFs as a vehicle for strengthening the ESDI was given further impetus by the Ministerial decisions of the North Atlantic Council in Berlin in June 1996. On this occasion the Ministers took an important qualitative step forward by agreeing that the ESDI would have to be developed within the Alliance. Hence they undertook to prepare, on the basis of sound military planning, for WEU-led operations based on the possible WEU use of NATO assets, including future CJTF Headquarters.

Since Berlin, the Alliance has been engaged in the detailed implementation of the decisions to develop a European option within NATO. This involves, among other things, identifying separable but not separate assets, capabilities and command elements needed for WEU-led operations. The Ministerial meeting of December 1996 gave further impetus to this work, which the Alliance hopes and expects to complete, along with a wide range of other internal adaptation measures, by the time of the Madrid Summit of July 1997.

CJTF: the concept

One important result of the Berlin Ministerial was the approval of the CJTF concept—in full: the report on an Overall Politico-Military Framework for the CJTF concept—over which Allied bodies had been labouring since 1994. This framework document not only represents an important milestone on the road towards actual CJTF implementation, but also a considerable conceptual investment in the future military operations of the Alliance.

Concerning the higher organisation of CJTF operations, the framework document underlines that the North Atlantic Council, with the advice of the Military Committee on military issues and supported by the Policy Coordination Group established in 1996, will maintain political control over NATO CJTFs. Second, the framework document specifies how CJTFs could be employed: to help the Alliance perform its missions, old and new, more efficiently; to support the ESDI; and to facilitate operations in which non-NATO countries participate. Taken together, these various requirements would constitute a tall order. More specifically, the variety of modes and circumstances foreseen for the employment of CJTFs will put great demands on the arrangements for commanding and controlling these task forces, that is to say on CJTF headquarters.

CJTF headquarters

In the CJTF framework document and in the documents that followed, much intellectual energy has been spent on the issue of CJTF headquarters. It is energy well spent, for we have witnessed since 1994 the gradual emergence of a real CJTF headquarters doctrine. In its most basic form this doctrine entails the following main features:

- a suitable *ad hoc* CJTF headquarters will be constructed around a multinational, joint nucleus selected from a range of permanently available nuclei embedded—mostly with dual-hatted personnel—in parent headquarters found in the current (and future) NATO military structure;
- these nuclei will provide the core of the key staff functions of a CJTF headquarters and will be augmented with the required additional personnel and with additional staff capabilities as needed; such Augmentation Modules will be drawn from other parent NATO headquarters, or from other appropriate multinational headquarters or national sources;
- a fully fledged CJTF headquarters will furthermore require the addition of Support Modules, that is specialised support units and elements of various types; these will be drawn from the same sources as the Augmentation Modules;
- each nucleus will be tasked with the preparation of its build-up. In addition, centralised CJTF headquarters planning will be conducted in a Combined Joint Planning Staff at the Major NATO Commander level. A Capabilities Coordination Cell will assist the Military Committee in providing planning guidance to the Major NATO Commanders and related advice to the North Atlantic Council.

The thus completed CJTF headquarters would then be able to take control of the units selected to make up the task force and to deploy to the theatre of operations.

Making the concept work

Due to the many requirements which the CJTF concept must satisfy, implementing the concept is more easily said than done. Clearly, making recommendations on the location, size, number and structure of CJTF headquarters elements and their *modus operandi* will require an evolutionary, trial-and-error approach. The NATO Military Authorities envisage three phases. In a first phase, the initial establishment of parent headquarters will allow the Major NATO Commanders to commence CJTF headquarters trials and exercises, thus creating the basis for an initial Alliance capability actually to deploy CJTF headquarters. The first CJTF headquarters trials are scheduled for the second half of 1997 and early 1998. To that end three initial Headquarters Nuclei have been set up. The second phase will be devoted to a thorough assessment of the Alliance's capability to deploy small and large-scale land- and sea-based CJTF headquarters. This assessment could, for instance, result in the designation of additional CJTF parent headquarters. The third and last phase should witness the full implementation of the CJTF concept, which will by then have to be adapted to the new NATO command structure. It goes without saying that experience gained from the rapid and highly effective deployment of the international Implementation Force (IFOR) in Bosnia-Herzegovina will be taken into account in all three phases of the CJTF implementation process.

WEU aspects

The creation of a CJTF capability for WEU-led operations is an integral part of the phased military implementation of the CJTF concept. The documents dealing with the CJTF concept as such and with its implementation elaborate on the WEU-specific aspects of CJTF, in line with the now firmly-rooted NATO-WEU cooperation on CJTF matters. In fact we are speaking of nothing less than a fully-fledged concept for WEU-led CJTF operations, a concept which of course should be fully consistent with and embedded in the military implementation of NATO's overall CJTF concept. The NATO Military Authorities are working on the development of such a concept as part of the overall CJTF implementation project. In order for them to complete their preparations for WEU-led CJTF operations, the NATO Military Authorities will, where needed, derive guidance from the work of the Policy Coordination Group on the development of the ESDI within the Alliance.

Happily, the main features of interest to the WEU are already falling into place. This is in part due to the fact that the 1994 Brussels Summit and especially the 1996 Berlin Ministerial meeting had already determined in quite some detail how the ESDI was to be built up within the Alliance and how full advantage should be taken of the CJTF concept to this end. I refer, of course, to the various taskings given by Allied Foreign and Defence Ministers in the context of NATO's internal adaptation process. These taskings are truly interrelated. The creation of the ESDI within NATO requires the elaboration of European command arrangements within NATO's new command structure capable of preparing, supporting, commanding and conducting operations under the political control and strategic direction of the WEU, and in doing so the creation of the ESDI within NATO also requires the need to incorporate fully the CJTF concept. Subsumed in this complex interrelationship is a host of further issues, some technical but some also political, that have arisen and continue to arise in the course of thinking through how the Alliance can help turn the ESDI into a reality without jeopardising the transatlantic partnership and NATO's integrated military structure. To name just the main issues on which work is progressing:

- military planning and exercises for illustrative missions identified by the WEU;
  terms of reference and the method of appointing a Deputy SACEUR with a view to his ESDI role;
- NATO-WEU information sharing arrangements for WEU-led operations;
  modalities for the release, monitoring and return of assets and capabilities made available to WEU;
- support from NATO's defence planning process for the conduct of WEU-led operations, and, last but not least, NATO-WEU consultations in the context of a WEU-led operation with NATO support.

I need not point out the complexity of NATO's internal adaptation process. Its various political, politico-military and military elements require careful orchestration if the desired result—ESDI as a living reality within NATO—is to be obtained. For the ESDI to become that living reality within NATO, Allied structures will in future have to be able to function either in an Atlantic or a European configuration. In the face of an emerging crisis, the switch from one configuration to the other will have to be made in a timely, flexible and decisive manner. In meeting this requirement, CJTF can make the difference in at least two ways. For CJTF is, all things considered, not only about providing the WEU with the indispensable means to mount operations under its leadership. In a more intangible but probably no less important way, CJTF can—by its very modular nature—instill in the Alliance the flexibility needed to act in whatever configuration circumstances will require.

This is all very well, yet at the end of the day the question still remains as to what a WEU-led CJTF would look like in practice. From the present state of the discussions, the following, albeit rough, picture emerges. At the request of the WEU, and after consultations in the North Atlantic Council, the Alliance could activate a CJTF Headquarters Nucleus for the WEU's use. This Nucleus would be completed with supporting Modules in much the same way as for a NATO-led CJTF operation. The task force itself, comprising forces that the WEU members had made available, would have a WEU commander and would be under the political control of the WEU. In addition to a CJTF headquarters, other NATO assets might also be transferred to the WEU for its temporary use, depending on the basis of consultations between the two organisations. Obviously, as of late April 1997, detailed military planning has not yet been completed. The practical modalities and arrangements which will be arrived at will also have to be tested in the course of trials and exercises. These will be governed by NATO standards and procedures.

Conclusion

To recapitulate the virtues of the concept: thanks to its inherent flexibility and cost-effectiveness, CJTF can meet the cumulative requirements of a reformed NATO, a greater European security and defence role, hands on political-military decision making and tight defence budgets. Not to be misunderstood, I should of course say that the ESDI cannot be realised at the push of a button, the button being CJTF. But CJTF does provide us with the tool that will help us deal with the challenges and opportunities of our new security environment.

PART III
NATO'S STRUCTURAL REFORM AND THE ESDI: A GOOD IDEA WASTED
GERT DE NOOY

G iving practical effect to a good idea through an organisation as hierarchical as NATO has proved as difficult as getting a super-tanker to change course. This task is certainly all the harder in view of the highly centrifugal forces that increasingly play on the Alliance's European, transatlantic and global ambitions. It also applies to the implementation of the decisions made´ at the NATO summit in January 1994. In retrospect, it must be said that the Allied policy makers were faced with a difficult task in producing a successful outcome. On the one hand, they had to take account of their own rhetoric in the years following the collapse of the Berlin Wall: phrases from the NATO communiqué such as 'Security in Europe is indivisible', 'The integrated military NATO structure offers the only guarantee of security in Central and Eastern Europe', and 'No new dividing lines' all raised high expectations among the USSR's one-time satellites, and the Visegrad states in particular hoped that to see these summit declarations followed by action. On the other hand, the summit also had to produce a survival strategy with three goals. The first concerned Alliance cohesion: both the United States and France had to reach agreement on the future of NATO. The second goal was a drastic and much-needed review of the NATO organisation and bureaucracy, a reorganisation which was already under way but now required to be reinvigorated and to acknowledge the developing European Security and Defence Identity. The third goal concerned the Alliance's credibility. With conflict still raging in the former Yugoslavia, NATO had to prove that it was still an effective security body. It is not surprising that the text of the summit declaration is rife with compro-

Commander Gert de Nooy, Royal Netherlands Navy, is Military Research Fellow at the Netherlands Institute of International Relations, Clingendael.

mises (particularly those struck between France and the United States) and its proposals open to varying interpretations.

In the event consensus, reflecting lowest-common-denominator agreement between the diverse aims of the 16 member states, was found to permit the summit to launch its major initiatives. Besides launching the Partnership for Peace (with participation in this offered as a substitute for NATO membership) and for introducing the American concept of counter-proliferation, attention focused on a politico-military *tour de force*: the idea of Combined Joint Task Forces (CJTF). This concept, in theory at least, offered the possibility of maintaining NATO's integrated military command structure while offering the West European nations the opportunity to operate independently outside the treaty area. However, in the last few years since 1994, the concept has been approached more from the point of view of its implications for NATO than of those for the Europeans. This brings us to what has until now been absent in the CJTF discussion; namely, considerations of the practical opportunities and implications of the concept with regard to the reinforcement of the European Security and Defence Identity (ESDI), the development of a common European defence policy and the formation of a combined European military force.

It is a sad fact that the CJTF concept—for it appears to be no more than an idea—has been given little concrete meaning since January 1994. The publications that exist on the concept's underlying politico-military significance are often contradictory. In particular, little light has been shed on the less abstract and more down-to-earth essentials of the concept, such as politico-military liabilities and responsibilities, the distribution of military advantages and disadvantages, the politico-military decision-making processes and risk and planning analysis for CJTF operations. The debate within NATO has been confined to the question of how to maintain the integrated military command structure in the face of a simultaneous development of *ad hoc* coalitions. The WEU has adopted a wait-and-see approach and limited itself to reacting to NATO proposals for the practical interpretation of the concept, and the focal point of the debate has come to rest on the use and deployment of

NATO staffs and headquarters in a CJTF role. Most of the studies which deal with this are not available to the public and are of a technical nature. Furthermore, even limited interpretation and development of a good idea have been thwarted by political differences among the Sixteen. In particular, France's delaying tactics have served to delay realisation of the CJTF concept. In order to keep sight of the practical advantages and disadvantages of the original idea, and to avoid the stalemate described above, a broad outline is given below of the opportunities offered by the CJTF concept, as originally intended, to strengthen the ESDI in European politico-military terms and of the implications for closer European military cooperation.

Prerequisites and principles

In the absence of a valid system of principles for the development of an operational planning concept, no military action should be contemplated. This is certainly true of operations which risk escalation, and hence threaten greater casualties. Since the level of force which will ultimately be used cannot be established in advance, allowance must be made for possible military losses during the course each CJTF operation, and the ability to retain the initiative should the situation escalate ('escalation dominance') must be maintained. In view of its liabilities and responsibilities, it is also essential that each government participating in the operation itself adheres to these principles itself. It is ultimately the responsibility of each government to justify its decisions concerning the armed forces on operations.

Planning and decision making

A set of principles for operational conceptual planning and decision-making is already developing and should be applied to all operations which can be carried out by a CJTF. It goes without saying that the importance of the principles will differ from case to case for each CJTF operation. The principles relate to the decision-making process concerning the actual deployment of military units. Some principles relate to politico-military analysis of contingencies in which European interests are at stake (clear-cut analysis of the assignment, accurate assessment of escalation potential). Some concern the military capacity needed to render the political aims successful (clear military objectives, suitability and timely availability of resources). However, the most important principles—those concerning the politico-military decision-making in respect to the CJTF deployments—are almost lost in the present discussion because of the emphasis on the concept's place in the restructuring of NATO headquarters.

Planning by a single staff

That planning for a CJTF operation should be conducted by a single staff is vital. The planning and execution of coalition operations are normally a matter of consensus. The issue here, however, is to give direction to military units which can conduct combat missions and for which minor disagreements over a plan of action could have disastrous consequences. To forestall the danger of these disagreements being transmitted down to the national units making up the Task Force, it is sensible to place the planning and management of the assignment in the hands of a single planning staff; one which is mission-tailored and which has understood working methods. This staff should also represent experience and expertise relevant to the assignment, function well as a team and the bulk or the totality of its members should ideally come from the same country. If it is also true to say that the country supplying the most troops for the CJTF has the greatest interest in the safe and effective execution of the mission, it also seems logical that this country should provide the staff responsible for the planning. The role specialisation that this approach presupposes would lead to designated potential 'Principal Force Providers' to be charged with responsibility for the planning and execution of certain categories of operation. If American interests were also at stake and the US were thus prepared to function as a 'Principal Force Provider', it would make sense for the Americans to take the lead in planning and execution.

Unambiguous political objectives

This principle should be a *sine qua non*, whatever the assignment. But because the objectives are usually determined by politics and often compromise politics at that, it is, unfortunately, also the principle which is most frequently departed from in practice. The requirement for unambiguous objectives, however, expresses the primacy of politics, and these objectives form the link between the political aims and the military feasibility of an assignment. Experience to date, for example in the former Yugoslavia and Somalia, has shown that nothing is as detrimental to a legitimising and authorising body as having its ambition frustrated. The inability to realise this ambition is due less to a lack of political will than to imprecise and ambiguous formulation of the political aims. Since political will, clearly defined political objectives and military capabilities are inextricably linked, all three elements should carry equal weight in determining the ultimate political aims of a CJTF mission.

Clear-cut political liability

The political responsibility (and the liability for any reverses) for a CJTF operation must be clearly defined before a start is made on the military planning. This responsibility is shared by the organisation authorising the operation (e.g. the UN, the OSCE, the EU) and the governments involved in the operational planning and execution. The political responsibility of the authorising organisation is four-fold. Firstly, it is responsible for the definition of political objectives. Secondly, it authorises the operation and thus approves the military details. Thirdly, it may be responsible for political negotiations with other parties involved. Fourthly, it bears responsibility for rounding off the operation once the objectives have been realised. The authorising organisation is not, however, responsible for the actual execution of the operations, neither for the command of the CJTF nor for the authority over resources and doctrine employed to achieve the military objectives. This responsibility rests entirely with the military planning staff. These planners must, however, obtain their political authorisation via the governments of the countries making a military contribution to the CJTF, a situation which gives rise to a complex relationship between political responsibility and liability. It is thus clear that many, if not all, force-providing member states of an authorising organisation need to be involved in the military planning and execution.

Remaining questions

Given the prerequisites and principles above, there remain a number of unanswered questions. These lie at the core of the theological controversy over the way ahead in CJTF affairs and they connect what is, in essence, a practical military idea both with its highly political character and more down-to-earth matters of implementation. Three key questions emerge.

The first question revolves around the relationship between the execution of contingency-specific Out-of-Area operations and the ongoing restructuring of an Integrated Military Structure still geared towards the more generic tasks of collective defence. After the Rome Summit of 1991, the Alliance began discussions on the reorganisation of NATO's defence planning system and its command and control structures. The introduction of the CJTF concept meant another drastic change of course in this reorganisation plan. As things stand, only a few national or NATO headquarters have available the planning and command facilities appropriate to the deployment of a large-scale CJTF of 30 000 troops or more. In the event of a European-led CJTF, the first problem will arise when troops and staff come to be separated from NATO's Article Five-based collective defence structure. Although the much-quoted Separable but not Separate might be politically desirable, it is not tenable in military terms: national forces are either part of the CJTF or part of the NATO IMS. In planning they may be double-hatted; in practice they are single-helmed. This in turn leads to the question of how these CJTFs are deployed and where and how the politico-military decision-making takes place, not to mention the military planning. One thing is certain: national headquarters staff will play a decisive role once European CJTFs start to be employed, and the Italian role in Operation Alba in Albania offers a recent example of this. A final problem in this context arises at the moment when a European CJTF has to be reintegrated smoothly into NATO's collective defence structure in cases when an Out-of-Area mission has escalated to the level of collective defence. This development is not wholly unlikely.

The second question has to do with the political responsibility and accountability of the Partnership for Peace states, should they provide military units to a CJTF. In this event non-NATO/WEU countries, considering their responsibilities for the lives of their personnel, are entitled to participation in the politico-military decision-making and the Command and Control of the CJTF mission. The actual deployment thus runs the risk of becoming ensnared in wrangling over staff appointment at the very time where flexibility and a sense of urgency are most needed: too many cooks spoil the broth. These questions, incidentally, leave aside that of the financial problems affecting both Alliance members and PfP Cooperation Partners when it comes to realising the CJTF concept on top of the existing costs of PfP and Alliance enlargement. Although CJTF is intended to offer new scope for Europe in the defence and security field, the parallel European project of monetary union (EMU) is compounding the squeeze caused by budget deficits and casting a shadow over this.

The last of the three questions is the most fundamental: when and where will CJTFs actually be deployed ? Until now the straightforward answer has been that this depends on the situation, and that each contingency will be assessed in the light of its own requirements. CJTFs could conceivably have been employed in Bosnia, Somalia, Rwanda, Zaïre and now Albania, but in each of these instances the requisite pieces were not in place for the miracle formula to be used. The WEU has shown a marked aversion to swinging its collective weight behind such minority initia-tives; moreover, its preference to date has been for low-level, low-risk commitments of a kind not requiring the full CJTF panoply to be brought into play. However, the Anglo-French-Dutch Rapid Reaction Force in Bosnia in 1995 and the Italian-led force deployed to Albania under Operation Alba forces are proof that the concept of Task Forces, Com-bined and Joint, much as originally intended, can be made to work even without being labelled as such. I conclude that NATO or WEU may as well adopt a different approach to security management, maybe akin to the legitimising approach we now see developing in the OSCE and the UN, and leave actual implementation to the countries whose main interests in the crisis are common. Whether NATO or the WEU finally and formally deploy CJTF in parts of Europe or its peripheries as envisaged will also be influenced by the prevailing attitude of Russia towards such intervention.

Conclusions

What can we conclude from the above? Accepting on the one hand the premise that the Europe of the future should be capable of standing on its own two feet and realising its political aims, where necessary in military terms, but acknowledging on the other that there exists today neither any single duly-constituted European political authority nor 'Eurosoldiers' at its disposal, it is argued that the deployment of CJTFs is best organised through a core group of European states. A core of six or seven European member states of NATO/WEU would seem to be the most appropriate for such a role, the states in question being France, Germany, the United Kingdom, Italy and the Benelux countries. These countries are in a position to form the defence and security motor of a future Europe in the promotion of collective interests, regardless of the size and number of its institutions. The present bilateral and multilateral military connections within this core group constitute both the foundation of this core and a point of departure for its further development which, it is emphasised, can only be realised in an organic, 'bottom up' manner. In order to further Europe's aims in the various contingencies that may arise, the military potential of the core group could be supplemented on a case-by-case basis with military resources from coalition partners who are prepared to make a contribution. The following division of labour within the core group is conceivable in this respect: the United Kingdom would lead tri-service projection missions aimed at maintaining the international rule of law in the far corners of the world; France and/or Italy would do the same in respect of missions projecting stability in the Western Mediterranean and to the South; Germany would take the lead for the direction of land-based operations relating to collective defence and the projection of stability to the East.

Where America's interests coincide with those of the core group, and the US is prepared to act as the major force provider, then it would make sense for the US to lead in the planning and execution. A force numbering 60 000 or so personnel would represent a major challenge, especially for a non-Article Five mission. It must be considered unlikely that a requirement on this scale would be answered by the Europeans alone; an emergency of this size would almost certainly elicit a combined response involving both Americans and Europeans. If, and only if, American and European resources fall short, a call could be made on the collective resources of NATO, which are by definition designed for the execution of the traditional NATO mission of Alliance collective defence. In the context of an OSCE mission, a more extensive coalition could be assembled with other European countries or multilateral organisations (perhaps the Commonwealth of Independent States) in order to promote stability in and around the OSCE area. It would make sense to allow military actions by such OSCE coalitions to be carried out in a NACC-plus context, whereby the coalition's strongest members would form the decision-making framework. This construction in stages would make it possible for the European core group of six actively to determine which course the EU (but also the OSCE) would sail in terms of military security and which political aims were attainable in an OSCE context.

The deciding criterion for the deployment of European CJTFs must be sound military capacity, rather the desire of Europe to prove its maturity. Should it transpire in generic planning that certain scenarios are not catered for, the military effort should consequently be stepped up to fill this shortfall. European CJTFs form the military foundations for policy in defence and military security policy, and these will come together on a case-by-case basis. Subject to a clear and common analysis by the Europeans of the contingency and an understanding of the military capacity available at a given moment, CJTF operations can be both formulated and carried out using the above principles and criteria for success.

PART IV: CJTF—MILITARY IMPLEMENTATION

IFOR AND LESSONS FOR FUTURE CJTFS
LIEUTENANT GENERAL MICHAEL JACKSON CB CBE

I have been impressed by the complexity and depth of the emerging CJTF doctrine, with its now-familiar refrain of 'separable but not separate'. It sometimes seems to me that we are embarked on a search for a Holy Grail, which, if found, would solve at a stroke all problems relating to the European dimension of collective security. In the meantime, while this remains elusive, it is practitioners such as myself who have to make things work as they are. And so I am grateful for the opportunity to put forward some thoughts concerning the practical military considerations of the CJTF concept.

The force headquarters

Table 1: CJTF HQ Functions

- *Planning deployment, employment and recovery*
- *Direction, control and coordination of operations*
- *Developing Courses of Action*
- *Preparing Operational Orders and Operational Plans*
- *Preparing Logistic Plans*
- *Keeping higher, adjacent and supporting commands informed*
- *Coordinating with other forces, governments and agencies*
- *Monitoring accomplishments*

Lieutenant General Michael Jackson CB CBE is Commander of NATO's ACE Rapid Reaction Corps (ARRC), the Alliance's strategic land reaction formation, which provided the Headquarters and many of the troop units for the NATO-led Peace Implementation Force (IFOR) in Bosnia-Herzegovina in 1996. During this period in Bosnia, General Jackson was Commander of the British-led Multinational Division South-West.

Table 1 shows the functions required of a CJTF headquarters, as defined in the draft NATO doctrine. Note the breadth and the depth of these functions, and what this means in terms of hard staff work and preparation—neither of which can be done at the drop of a hat.

Table 2: CJTF HQ Capabilities

- *Rapid formation and deployment to the Area of Operations, with:* (a) *Leading elements deployed within seven days of the Action Order*

  (b) *Follow-on elements available within 15 days*
- *Exercising Command & Control of NATO and non-NATO forces*
- *Communication with higher, supporting and subordinate commands; civil authorities; International and Non-Governmental Organisations*
- *Receiving and disseminating intelligence*
- *Self-sustainment for 30 days*
- *Local self-protection of personnel, equipment and information*

The same may be said of the capabilities demanded of a CJTF HQ, laid out in Table 2. The Headquarters, of course, is no more than precisely that—a Commander with his essential staff and communicators. Such a headquarters can, of course, plan in peacetime, but it cannot operate without a force structure. There is as yet no firm doctrine on force generation, or force employment once in theatre.

I will have more to say about readiness, but I would emphasise at this stage that for the lead elements to be ready to go in seven days, with the remainder in 15, is a very considerable demand. IFOR, of course, was put together in the autumn of 1995, when the CJTF concept was still in embryo. It is fair to say that the way in which IFOR was assembled has some parallels with how a CJTF might be generated: the theatre headquarters (HQ IFOR) was drawn from an existing NATO headquarters, namely HQ AFSOUTH, which could therefore be said to have produced the nucleus. This nucleus was then augmented as required. Subordinate to the CJTF HQ are the component commanders for Land, Sea, Air, Special Forces and Logistics, each with their own headquarters and command structure. Using Bosnia again as an illustration, it was as the Land Component Headquarters that HQ ARRC was deployed.

In the context of readiness, it is instructive to reflect briefly on what happened at the end of HQ ARRC's year in theatre. In terms of a deployable Corps-level formation HQ at high readiness, the ARRC is a one-shot weapon within NATO—which is why there are thoughts that the Alliance could make good use of a second Rapid Reaction Corps HQ. But in the absence of a second such HQ, NATO was obliged in the Autumn of 1996 to create an *ad hoc* theatre and land component headquarters to replace HQ ARRC. This was done from HQ LANDCENT, a static headquarters not designed to be deployable—unlike the ARRC. The process of defining the structure of this HQ and apportioning posts to the various nations was not without difficulty.

The advent of CJTF HQs will go a long way to minimise such difficulties. But they will not be eradicated altogether: the CJTF HQ nuclei to be embedded within static NATO HQs do not identify by person the Commander, nor in every case his Chief of Staff. The Deputy Chief of Staff is nominated, along with his permanent planning team of some 20-30 staff. What this means is that the Commander, and often his Chief of Staff, will only be nominated in the immediate run-up to the operation itself and are therefore unknown until deployment—although I accept that in reality there will be some inspired guesswork. I recognise the reasons behind this, but it makes me uneasy in purely military terms.

Aims and planning

I turn now to identify those lessons from IFOR which I believe have relevance to CJTF planning and operations.

The End-State. It may seem paradoxical to begin with the question of the end-state, but strange as it may seem enough, this is exactly where you must start. What is it that you are going to do? More important still, who is going to define what it is that you are going to do, and how will the judgement be made that you have achieved it? In this context, the Bosnian case is not a particularly good example of how to define an end-state. In my view, the proper end-state of the Dayton process must be an objective judgement that the conditions have been set for a lasting peace.

Let me elaborate. The Dayton Agreement has many strands. There are eleven annexes, only one of which is purely military. If any of these interconnected, intertwined and mutually supporting strands fails to deliver its own part of the end-state, the whole of the end-state may be at risk and indeed may fail. Annex 1-A required IFOR initially to separate the warring factions, to put them back into barracks, to demobilise them to some extent, and to subject them to a very close monitoring process. Also in Annex 1-A was the installation of a Zone of Separation along what is now the Inter-Entity Boundary Line. The end-state of the Military Annex can therefore be defined as the achievement of an atmosphere of military security, not peace *per se*, but a removal of the possibility of further fighting, to allow all the other actors (not least, the parties themselves) to bring together the other strands to produce the overall end-state. By D+120 in late April, the military provisions of Annex 1-A were complete. In addition to maintaining military security, the purpose thereafter—not specifically stated, but made utterly clear by mission analysis—was, where possible, to assist the other agencies in contributing to the end-state. If this meant lending a hand to the elections, for example, or in assisting rehabilitation, that seems to me to be entirely sensible and wholly laudable. Some described this as Mission Creep, a phrase I abhor. I have already said that, to me, the overall end-state criterion for success in Bosnia is the setting of conditions for a lasting and self-sustaining peace. Whether that is achievable or not under the Dayton Agreement must remain for the present a matter of personal judgement.

Pre-Deployment Exercises. The desirability of exercising together *before* deployment is self-evident, but again, if you are going to put an operation together on an *ad hoc* basis, this becomes difficult to plan. We often hear about the virtues of ad-hockery as against institutionalisation.

My belief is that neither of these is particularly attractive in its extreme form, and that the correct course probably lies somewhere between the two. There is a limit to what soldiers, sailors and airmen can reasonably be expected to put together virtually overnight and make succeed. I emphasise the last point, since failure is not an option.

Force generation

We now come to the generation of the Force itself. An Article Five operation, considered in this context, is relatively simple. On the other hand, if we do not all feel fundamentally threatened, as is likely to be the case under circumstances *less* than Article Five, the glue that binds us together as Alliance members is, in some respects, weakened. As a result, should the need arise to put together a coalition force structure for a non-Article Five contingency, this will a be a coalition of the willing made up of countries from the Alliance, and possibly (as with IFOR/SFOR) from countries outside NATO. The impossibility of knowing in advance where units and specialists will come from creates its own difficulties, not least in terms of planning and training.

The Statement of Requirement; the Resource Process and Force Contributions. Once the Commander has been given the military problem, he draws up an estimate of the forces required, and decides on an appropriate Order of Battle for the task in hand. This may sound fairly straightforward, but placed in a multinational context (particularly one for a non-Article Five operation), matters quickly enter the tortuous and Byzantine process of nations deciding which forces they are prepared to offer, and very often the constraints under which they are prepared to offer them. A national capital may respond with: Yes, we will come, but provided we are under command of A, or not under command of B, or provided we can go to area C and not to area D. Many nations, often for understandable reasons but sometimes not, surround their offers of troop contributions with conditions of this kind—and reconciling them all is not easy. Producing deployment and troops-to-task plans which take account of these national sensibilities but yet make operational sense, is inevitably something of a juggling act. Moreover, the glamorous tasks are usually popular; that other tasks are unglamorous or comparatively more danger-ous is quickly made obvious by the fact that nations are reluctant to take them on. The reality is that the Commander may have to allocate tasks to troops rather than the reverse.

Certification. Should a Task Force and its Commander take a troop contribution, from whatever source, merely at face value? Some form of reassurance is called for, and Certification is a quality control mechanism that allows the commander to satisfy himself that he will not be let down. A force contribution is thus *certified*—and I accept that this is an unfortunate expression—as being efficient.

Force deployment

Force Posture; National Deployment Execution and Restrictions. Let us assume that we have a Headquarters and we have a Force. These now have to deploy to the theatre of operations. The posture that force elements adopt, both on arrival and subsequently, is also something that varies according to national perspectives and national military culture. IFOR was congratulated on having avoided suffering any casualties due to enemy action. This is true, but experience has shown that different nations will vary as to how much importance they attach to this question of Force Protection. This is not just an academic argument. Some may say that Force Protection is the most important aspect, whereas others will say that this should be Mission Accomplishment. The appreciation of risk, and the acceptance of risk, will therefore vary. This is something that is not always easily managed in a multinational force. I have already referred to national restrictions of this kind above.

Readiness. Table 3 overleaf gives an indication of Reaction Times, and by extension what Readiness really means. The top line represents Cold War NATO procedure, but these procedural hurdles make sound sense. On the second line are the actual dates involved in the IFOR deployment. In this case the Warning and the Request for Action arose on the same day—11 October—as the Dayton Agreement came on the horizon. I acknowledge that NATO and the ARRC had had a long time to prepare, and much work

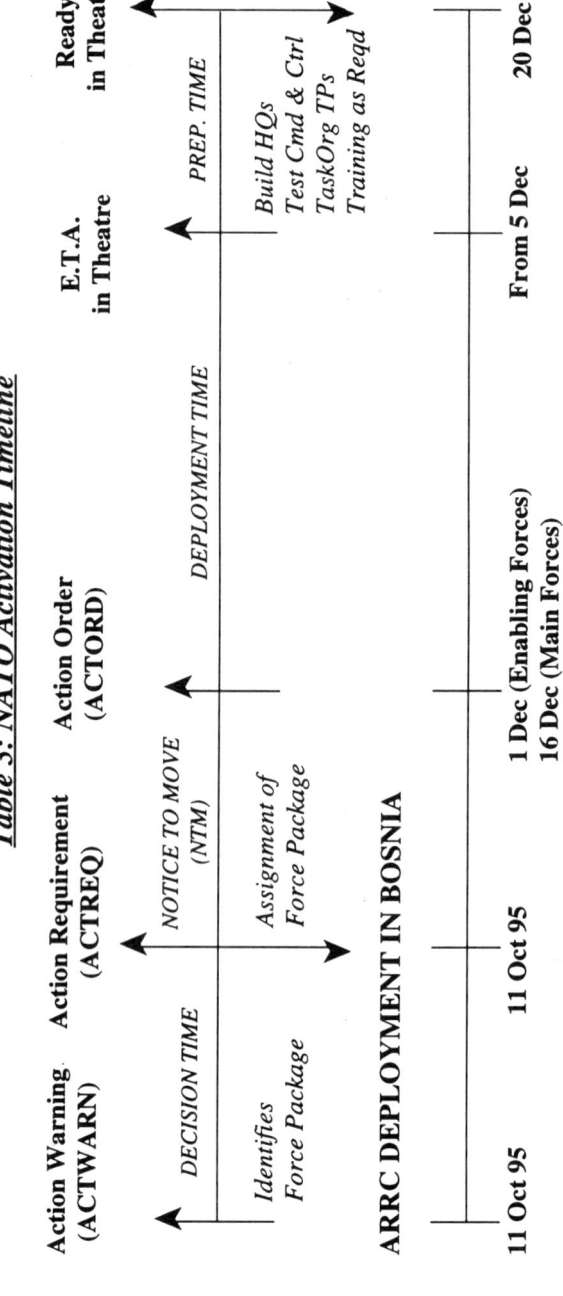

Table 3: NATO Activation Timeline

had already gone into planning, but events nonetheless came at a considerable rush. The actual executive Action Order for Enabling Forces* was on 1 December, with a few fingers doubtless crossed that everything would come together, because it was only on 16 December that the peace accords (which were after all only initialled at Dayton) were signed into a fully-fledged treaty, the General Framework Agreement for Peace. D-Day, as it is known to the military, was to be four days later, on 20 December. Table 3 shows the compression of time that took place as D-Day got nearer, and how very little time we had once the Dayton Agreement was finally delivered. Getting the ARRC ready under this pressure called for more than a little heroic improvisation, and once again, I make the point that this work was put in by a ready-formed, up-and-running headquarters. I leave it to readers to imagine for themselves the practicality of achieving a reaction time of this kind with even more ad-hockery, such as if the Headquarters does not exist until D minus 30 and only assembles for a particular operation.

Command and control

The suitability of present NATO command arrangements; Unity of Effort. NATO uses command states of considerable complexity and nuanced definition which were designed for the Cold War and for the General Deployment Plan (GDP), drawn up in that age of relative certainty before 1989. There are many who feel—and I am one of them—that these Command States have more than outlived their useful lives and offer too much room for manoeuvre and hedging of bets. Put simply, if the Commander on the ground does not have adequate command authority, there is the constant risk that the operation will fray. For this reason, we have fallen back upon talking about Unity of Effort rather than Unity of Command, because there were occasions in IFOR when the appropriate method was to exhort—rather than order—people to go in the same direction for the common good. Relating this to the CJTF concept, the fact

---

* This term usually implies a Special Forces presence to prepare ground prior to the arrival of the main force. *(Editor's note)*

that the Commander of the force and his Chief of Staff are not nominated until something happens and military operations are in prospect increases the scope for complications in this area.

Logistics

Logistics remain unglamorous as ever, but without them no operation will cross its Line of Departure. NATO's bedrock in this area is the document known as MC 319, which, perhaps more in hope for the moment than in reality, looks towards the increased multinationalisation— if I dare use that word—of Logistics. But nations are, understandably, very careful about relying on anybody else for medical cover, for example, for their own soldiers. The consequence of this reticence is the continued existence of national stove-pipes, the soldier's term for those parallel and duplicative national channels along which come the beans and the bullets. Logistic friction is an amalgam of both materiel and psychological factors. At the end of the day, nations are very wary indeed of laying themselves open to domestic criticism. For example, should a soldier die because his injuries were not treated quickly enough by another nation's medical organisation, or should troops be without proper boots because foreign suppliers have failed to meet their contractual obligations, political difficulties quickly loom at home. There is also the technical problem that very often equipment belonging to different nations is simply not interoperable. Multinational logistic arrangements may therefore be effective, but they are not necessarily efficient.

Interoperability. Progress in this area remains disappointing. While present fuel and, in some cases, ammunition interchangeability is relatively straightforward (and arrangements, known as mutual assistance, were put in place between national contingents in Bosnia), the situation regarding spare parts is still very difficult. That said, as IFOR went on, people got used to being able to operate together; they learnt about the art of the possible and kept pushing further at it to improve logistic interoperability. However, and it has been said before, much progress remains to be made.

NATO funding and Host Nation Support contracting procedures. This last point is vitally important. In any operation there will be money involved, and probably large amounts of it. NATO already has a system of funding in being, and the combination of muscle and credibility appropriate to a long-established organisation with powerful members. Any future sub-group or coalition contemplating military operations and contracting Host Nation Support will need to ponder whether it can deliver its cash and its contracting in the same relatively efficient manner.

Support to civilian agencies

For Peace Support Operations, the question of effective interaction with the many non-military actors on the stage assumes vital importance. There is a plethora of International and Non-Governmental Organisations likely to be involved in a Peace Support Operation, and with whom good liaison and interaction is most important. The IOs and NGOs are independent bodies and can understandably seem jealous of their own autonomy, but this civil-military liaison is vital if you are all to be going in the same direction. Not only does this take up additional manpower, but it must be high-quality manpower, since the people needed are good officers who can operate largely on their own and pull things together.

Multinational operations

Multinationality lies at the core of both the IFOR experience and the CJTF concept of operations, whether at the political or military level. It must be stated firmly that it is a delusion to assume that multinationality is some form of force multiplier in military terms. It is not. It brings with it friction, national agendas and the requirement to spend a lot of time keeping people united. That said, provided that the political advantages of multinationality outweigh the military friction, its benefits are clear. But while the political advantage by and large rests elsewhere, it is up to the military to work at it on the ground so as to ensure that multinationality actually delivers its benefits. There is no reason to be gloomy about this, since multinationality is rightly here to stay. My own ARRC headquarters is multinational, and this is a factor which demands constant and careful attention. Predictably, I would emphasise that the framework nation concept that we employ in the ARRC strikes a very good balance, capitalising on the political advantage while minimising the military friction which multinationality necessarily entails.

Conclusion: Peace Support Operations Doctrine

I conclude, briefly, on the question of Peacekeeping as against Peace Enforcement. Many commentators have touched on the difficulties in which UNPROFOR found itself, in particular in 1993-94, whereby a force equipped and mandated for Peacekeeping found itself being dragged down the path of Peace Enforcement. The results I think we all know. There is a moral to be found in this tale. It is this: if—and only if—you are confident that you have the consent of all sides (however many there may be) and that that consent will not evaporate at some point in the future, then you can enter on a Peacekeeping basis, i.e. lightly-armed, with fairly tight rules of engagement, and operating on the basis of that consent. If, however, you do not have that consent, or you have the slightest fear that it may be withdrawn, wisdom demands that you enter with a Peace Enforcement capability, so that you can escalate if need be. The very fact that you have this capacity to retain the upper hand in any escalation may mean that it is not necessary to put it into effect, because the very deterrent effect of a muscular presence will achieve the desired aim. I think that as NATO refines the CJTF concept and the opportunities it offers for European-led operations, we need to dwell hard and carefully on that UNPROFOR lesson and its moral in terms of scales of operation.

PART IV
CJTF OPERATIONS: AN AMERICAN PERSPECTIVE
LIEUTENANT COLONEL CHARLES BARRY

It is a daunting challenge to draw lessons from a single experience, particularly one that is not yet over. I am reminded of the anecdote about Secretary of State Henry Kissinger and Chinese Premier Chou-en-Lai. Asked by Kissinger what he believed to be the lessons of the French Revolution, Chou allegedly replied that it was still too soon to tell. We should be cautious about drawing initial lessons from Bosnia, partly because it is so recent and partly because it is but one experience.We are going to want to add many other experiences to our data-base, before deciding where to take CJTF. Nonetheless, CJTF is in front of us and there are decisions to be made by all nations, not only affecting politics but also resources. Forces are being drawn down and military planners need to take informed decisions about the forces we shall need in future. The CJTF concept, whether in relation to NATO or the WEU, will go a long way to answering these questions.

I speak as an American. As the United States looks around the world, we need to know what forces will be kept deployed forward, what forces we must plan to deploy from the US, and what kind of operations we need to prepare for. To a certain extent, these factors are central to our concept for participating in NATO activities—exercises, training and Partnership for Peace (PfP)—in peacetime, and in positioning ourselves to be ready to respond to crises. Of course, the US forces earmarked for collective defence will be different, more robust and conventional. However, CJTFs can and will be committed for Article Five missions as well. That was agreed at Brussels in 1994 and again since that time. For all these reasons, CJTFs and the way in which thinking on them is influenced by experience in Bosnia, is being carefully considered in Washington at

Lt. Col. Charles Barry is Senior Military Fellow at the National Defense University's Institute for National Strategic Studies, Fort McNair, in Washington DC.

several levels. Linking this, in passing, to PfP, it is true that we made significant strides in bringing some 19 Partnership nations on board in IFOR and SFOR. However, they should not be misled; in actual fact, a lot of them were carried by NATO.

While CJTFs can be used for Article Five missions inside NATO's borders, it is beyond them that they are most likely to be employed. The CJTF concept itself is not new. What is new is that we are attempting to institutionalise, on a multinational basis, a concept heretofore mainly associated with *ad hoc* coalitions. The reason we are doing this is militarily sound. It is the preservation of our forces in conditions of contingency crisis response at short notice and over long lines of communications. Today we must be able to use fewer forces for more purposes. Simply put, the CJTF concept is the only way to effect operations where our collective interests are potentially at risk, beyond our borders. Therefore we have to look at how we are going to bring CJTF together.

The absence of approved NATO doctrine for CJTF is a crucial shortcoming. How the CJTF is employed must be planned and practised through training and exercises, not only within NATO but also in the WEU, and indeed at national level as well. Doctrine, that is, how to resource, deploy and employ a CJTF, has to be developed and taught, all the way down to the fundamental military schooling that many of our people undergo. We must not make this too complex. We have been doing these kinds of operations for a very long time. I spent two-thirds of my military career in XVIII Airborne Corps, serving as a member of various Task Forces at either Brigade, Division or Corps level depending on the mission. We were so accustomed to putting together task forces that we almost never deployed as any other formation. Of course, land force-based Task Forces are the easiest to visualise, but keep in mind that there are air and maritime Task Forces as well.

The US has a lot of experience in joint matters, but US doctrine is thin when it comes to combined operations. This disparity exists because US forces have not had to work with allies in a fully multilateral context. The US has usually been cast so heavily in the role of coalition lead nation that allied forces have been essentially appended to this US force. Americans, in such formations, modify their procedures little from that used in a purely US operation. For NATO CJTFs, the US will have to learn more about multilateral procedures, especially since the same doctrine will have to be shared by NATO and the WEU. We therefore need to go much further in the doctrine area. NATO has produced some rudimentary documents regarding Peace Support Operations. However, these documents have not yet received approval at a level above SHAPE, for political reasons, and insufficient objectives have been set for exercises in peace operations and crisis response.

Lessons from Bosnia

I now turn to our experience in Bosnia. This operation has exposed the limits of national responsibilities for logistics. It is very difficult to take NATO's logistics system, that was designed to fold in upon itself in defence of Alliance territory and to be supported with interior lines of communication, and project it beyond NATO's borders. The limitations of the old system become particularly evident over long distances. There is both a lack of interoperability to some extent—particularly with respect to repair parts—and at the same time a widespread resistance to entrust logistics to other countries. Commanders always want to command their own logistic support, and this mindset has to be overcome. For small nations, in particular, a new system must be developed. In future we are likely to see logistic support, continuing to be provided on a national basis where essential and practicable, but augmented by a lead nation or agency responsible for the needs of groups of nations, at least concerning commodities that are difficult to transport or store.

Another issue highlighted in Bosnia—and elsewhere—is the influence of the media on modern military operations. We were less aware of this during the Cold War. In Bosnia, not only are most military operations 'on camera', but the local factions quickly learned how to use the media to further their agendas. Also, the daily press briefings in Sarajevo, at HQ IFOR and HQ ARRC, immediately added to the pressure put on commanders when things went astray. To carry the point about openness a stage further, much of IFOR's operational correspondence was necessarily classified 'NATO Confidential/NATO Secret—Releasable to IFOR'; i.e. releasable to Russia and other nations to which these things would not previously have been released. Much of that same information became available to the press. Both NATO and the WEU will have to get used to this level of shared information in future operations. And we shall still want effective protection for certain information against non-NATO recipients.

Another lesson is that the Alliance has far to go regarding expertise in civil-military relations. Unlike our European Allies, the US has Brigades of civil-military personnel whose primary mission is to set up a Civil-Military Operations Centre (CMOC) next to the Tactical Operations Centres, so that civilians can come and find out about operations, coordinate refugee flows, etc. In Bosnia, the military are having to perform a whole additional level of civilian-military coordination, participating in civil-military commissions, provisional election commissions and other bodies. At every level, from Battalion to HQ IFOR, there are civil-military structures to be manned, and in most cases run, by the military. The available personnel are almost all US, and their numbers are inadequate. Even these had to be retrained to deal with organisations like OSCE, the High Representative's Office and so on. The shortfall, moreover, is not just in civil-military relations, but also military-military relations. A huge investment in liaison teams was necessary, and, besides linguistic abilities, they all needed communications, transport and equipment.

In the past, once a political decision had been taken, the politicians turned the operation over to the military authorities to execute. In Bosnia— and I submit that this will be repeated in future CJTF operations, whether run by NATO, the WEU or some other coalition—the politicians followed the operation down to the battlefield, staying with the military day-by-day, and not simply looking over the commander's shoulder, but giving detailed guidance to fine-tune the political impact in-theatre and at home. Ambassador Frowick, Carl Bildt and many others stayed with us throughout the operation. There is now a much tighter level of control on the military purpose and a desire to influence minor military action to get a specific political result. This causes commanders to know much more about the political context of their operation than has been required before. The competence of soldiers is extremely important, not only because of their complex equipment, but also in view of the complexity of the mission. Up against a Serb, a Croat, or a Bosnian crowd, soldiers need to understand the differences and the roots of the conflict. This requires us to maintain a high intelligence level in our forces. Of course, our prime concern by far is for the lives and personal safety of our soldiers, but added to this is the knowledge that they are very expensive to train and take time to replace

It was imperative in Bosnia to maintain momentum. We deliberately moved in with continuous momentum and we kept the clock ticking for one requirement after another, to keep the factions off-balance and unable to counter our activities with initiatives of their own. Initiative, an old Principle of War, was thus exploited for a new purpose. Good Intelligence and Communications helped us maintain that momentum. The use of overhead systems, the use of Remotely Piloted Vehicles and the robust automation of headquarters were very important. At the same time, we found the military unwilling to accept total reliance on automation: behind many computers, for example, you could still find a map with grease-pencil marks. We have some way to go in automation, and one of the key complaints was the spread of computer viruses. The PowerPoint Rangers, as we called them, staff officers who would prepare slides for briefings, would slip slides from one computer to another, and many viruses were transferred in this way.

Operating in Bosnia has also underscored the versatility of the helicopter. The attack helicopter provides an intimidating presence, as is well-known, but the night and infra-red capability was also crucial to the intelligence effort. We may see greater demand for airmobile forces, not limited to the attack function, but also for Command and Control and Logistics. It was useful for acquainting commanders with outlying areas, for logistics and medical evacuation, and simply for showing presence. These indicate to me that emphasis may shift away from heavy forces and that helicopters may come more to the fore. However, there are always trade-offs. Helicopters are still maintenance-intensive and weather-dependent to some degree, and in many cases they can still be susceptible to ground fire.

Conclusion: CJTF and ESDI

Although the term is relatively new in NATO, CJTF is quite straightforward: Combined and Joint simply mean the synergy of our collective resources; land, sea and air brought together multinationally, because we are all short of forces. A Task Force is task-tailored. It will, hopefully, be designed up-front in macro terms, but some elements will need to be tailored and some last-minute *ad hoc* arrangements made. This last minute tailoring can be anticipated and trained for to some degree. After all, we are adopting the concept so as to be able to respond to crises rapidly and flexibly. We are therefore unable to define the CJTF's specific tasks in advance. There is, though, a hidden limit to Task Force operations that is not often discussed: they pull resources from existing organisations. Operation Provide Comfort, for example, pulls a General officer and pilots from their normal duties and sends them to Turkey for six months, which means that other jobs are not being performed and that the money being used to do this is being pulled out of other units. You can only do this for a limited time. If Bosnia lasts several years, it is probably going to be necessary to set up a standing, non-Task Force, command with its own budget and personnel lines and so forth. That is something we have yet to face.

I finish with the ESDI, which is in an altogether different category. It is a phenomenon that cannot be defined adequately in other terms, even by Europeans. We see its many manifestations. I consider the ESDI as the umbrella term covering everything that is collectively European in the fields of security and defence: the CFSP as its political expression; the WEU as its institutional expression; the Eurocorps as a military formation that expresses it, the Mostar and Danube operations as operational expressions of it, the efforts in armaments cooperation, and so on. It is an evolving identity, the spillover from integration in other areas. But, from an American perspective, the ESDI discussion can still seem perplexing. We are anxious to see how we are to reforge our relationship with our European Allies for the future. We look out anxiously to see what it is that the ESDI will actually unveil. What is this identity? We have many other theatres to deal with, and our forces are shrinking. As the US draws down, with the indications of the upcoming quadrennial defence review that more will be drawn away from Europe, we wonder about the sort of ESDI that will allow our interests in Europe to be protected by Europeans.

It is not clear. It is not clear to us that the Europeans have a common idea of this European identity. If there is anything that we can point to, it is the origin of the WEU's own reawakening. That event in 1984 was triggered by three motivations in Europe. First, the desire to be prepared in the event Europe could no longer count on the US for its protection. Second, the desire to have more influence in European affairs, and third, a logical desire to expand cooperation from the economic arena to that of security. Each of these three rationales continues to motivate proponents of ESDI today. I do not know that Washington is all that happy to see this European identity emerge; there seems, public declarations notwithstanding, to be some scepticism. We Americans watch to see whether this ESDI will be healthy for the transatlantic relationship or erode it, even though to some extent America is being not as helpful as it could.

With respect to the question of CJTF as a lifeline for a European defence policy: CJTF can help, but it cannot reverse-engineer this. The ESDI is a function of the political will to make it a reality. CJTF will make it stronger. But let no-one fool themselves that it is enough to take NATO resources in the belief that this will give Europe the political will that it has yet to find.